Workbook

Administrative Office Management
Complete Course
THIRTEENTH EDITION

Pattie Odgers, Ed.D.

Coconino Community College

Flagstaff, AZ

THOMSON

SOUTH-WESTERN

Australia · Canada · Mexico · Singapore · Spain · United Kingdom · United States

THOMSON
⁕
SOUTH-WESTERN ™

Administrative Office Management, Complete Course, 13th edition

Pattie Odgers

VP/Editorial Director:
Jack W. Calhoun

VP/Editor-in-Chief:
Dave Shaut

Senior Publisher:
Karen Schmohe

Acquistions Editor:
Joseph Vocca

Project Manager:
Penny Shank

Consulting Editor:
Sharon Massen

Production Manager:
Patricia Matthews Boies

Production Editor:
Colleen A. Farmer

VP/Director of Marketing:
Carol Volz

Marketing Manager:
Lori Pegg

Marketing Coordinator:
Georgi Wright

Manufacturing Coordinator:
Kevin Kluck

Internal Designer:
ElectroPub

Compositor:
ElectroPub

Printer:
Westgroup

For permission to use material from this text or product, submit a request online at http://www.thomsonrights.com. Any additional questions about permissions can be submitted by email to thomsonrights@thomson.com.

For more information contact South-Western, 5191 Natorp Boulevard, Mason, Ohio, 45040. Or you can visit our Internet site at: http://www.swlearning.com

The names of all companies or products mentioned herein are used for identification purposes only and may be trademarks or registered trademarks of their respective owners. South-Western disclaims any affiliation, association, connection with, sponsorship, or endorsement by such owners.

TABLE OF CONTENTS

Introduction to The Activity Workbook

The Activity Workbook is designed to help you become personally involved and to participate more directly in your study of administrative office management. The different assignments simulate on-the-job experiences found in offices of all sizes. The wide-ranging assignments, which complement your textbook and your instructor's presentation, will make you more aware of administrative management principles, policies, and practices.

The Activity Workbook contains the following kinds of activities and projects:

• *Review Activity* that can help you define what you remember from reading the chapter.

• *Practical Experience Assignments* that include projects in self-analysis, field investigation, and case studies.

• *Internet Research Assignments* that underscore the notion that information changes so quickly that one of the best sources for current updates to the textbook and management practices are through all-embracing exploration and use of the Internet.

• *Hands-on Computer Assignments* that present real management type computer applications that administrative managers can be called upon to perform from time to time using word processing and spreadsheet software. Throughout the Activity Workbook, a disk symbol will appear next to the project title if the project is on the Data CD. The files are prepared in Office 97 using Microsoft Word for word processing projects and Microsoft Excel for spreadsheet projects.

For many of these projects, you, the student, will assume the role of Ms. RosaLee Saikley, administrative office manager (AOM) at a business consulting firm called International Business Services. As the AOM, you will have more than ten office workers reporting to you most of the time.

International Business Services is a medium-size consulting firm in Phoenix, Arizona, and has more than 100 clients it serves on a regular basis. Approximately 12 consultants specialize in two areas of consulting—computer-related issues and human relations concerns. Below is the current organizational chart for International Business Services.

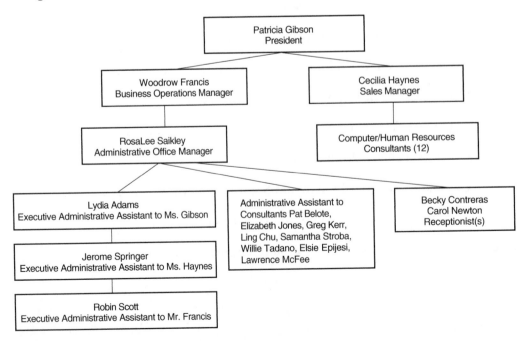

CHAPTER 1

THE EVOLUTION OF MANAGEMENT PRACTICES

REVIEW ACTIVITY

PROJECT 1-1: Matching Terminology

Directions: In the Answers column, write the letter of the item in Column 1 that is most often associated with each item in Column 2.

Column 1	Column 2	Answers
A. Administrative management	1. The father of scientific management	1. ____
B. Administrative manager	2. Result from experiences that create positive attitudes toward work and arise from the job content itself	2. ____
C. Frederick W. Taylor	3. Related to the word administration, which describes the performance of, or carrying out of, assigned duties	3. ____
D. Henry Fayol		
E. Motivators	4. Creates a future for the organization and includes 9 phases	4. ____
F. Chain of command	5. The management function of devising ways and means of ensuring that planned performance throughout the process is actually achieved	5. ____
G. Strategic planning process		
H. Organizing	6. The person responsible for planning, organizing, and controlling the information processing activities and for leading people in attaining the organization's objectives	6. ____
I. Controlling		
J. Principles	7. Shows the authority-responsibility relationships that link superiors and subordinates throughout the entire organization	7. ____
	8. First management author to state a series of management principles that would become guidelines for successful coordination	8. ____
	9. Broad, general statements that are considered to be true and that accurately reflect real-world conditions in all walks of life	9. ____
	10. The multifaceted management function that gets things done	10. ____

PRACTICAL EXPERIENCE ASSIGNMENTS

PROJECT 1-2: Analyzing the Span of Control

Span of control refers to the number of employees who are directly supervised by one person. A basic principle of management states that the span of control should be limited to a manageable number. Among other factors, the span of control is related to the type of direction and control exercised over the workers and the latitude extended them in decision making.

Directions: Two different spans of control are illustrated in Charts 1-1 and 1-2. As you see, a wide span of control creates a flat structure, while a narrow span of control creates a tall structure. After you have studied the charts, indicate below each chart the office conditions under which the span of control would be an appropriate organization pattern.

Chart 1-1

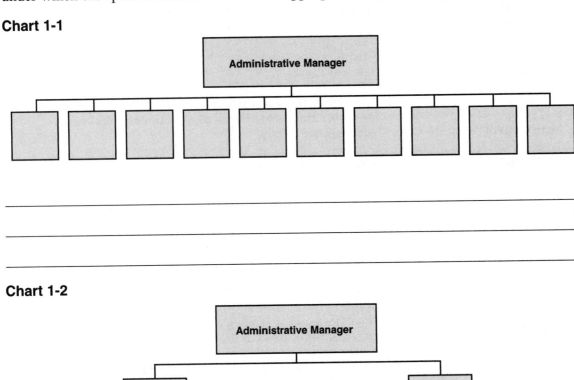

_____

_____

_____

Chart 1-2

_____

_____

_____

PROJECT 1-3: A Philosophy of Administrative Management

For some, one of the objectives of studying administrative management is to develop a philosophy of management. For others, the study will aid in refining and more clearly defining their philosophy. It will be rewarding from time to time during this course to sit back and reflect upon your own beliefs, concepts, and attitudes regarding the process of administrative management in the workplace.

As a first step in your thinking about a philosophy of administrative management, we shall examine a classification of leadership styles offered by the behavioral school of management thought. These leadership styles will provide you with an analytical tool that can be used in producing successful leadership.

Five leadership styles have been identified and defined:

1. *Autocratic leader.* The autocratic leader, or authoritarian leader, rules with unlimited authority. This is the AM who "tells" rather than "sells" or "consults." This leader keeps the bulk of the power and influence in the decision-making process to himself or herself. Thus, those who report to an autocrat are provided little, if any, motivation to engage in problem solving or in decision making at their levels.

2. *Bureaucratic leader.* This leader sets and follows fixed rules; a hierarchy of authority; and rigid, formal routines. The AM viewed as a bureaucrat "tells" workers what to do. The basis for the AM's orders are the policies, procedures, and rules of the organization.

3. *Diplomatic leader.* The diplomatic leader is skillful in helping people solve their problems or meet the needs of a particular situation. This manager is expert in employing tact and conciliation and rarely arouses hostility among workers. The diplomatic AM prefers "selling" rather than "telling" people he or she manages by persuasion and individual motivation. Workers are usually provided some freedom to react, to question, to discuss, and even to present arguments that support their views.

4. *Participative leader.* This leader openly invites workers to join in and take part in making decisions, setting policies, and analyzing methods of operation. Some participative AMs are democratic and let their workers know in advance that the group's decision, usually arrived at by consensus or majority vote, will be binding. Other participative AMs are consultative, and although they invite involvement, discussion, and recommendations from the group, they make it clear that they alone are accountable and reserve the final decision.

5. *Free-rein leader.* The free-rein leader sets goals and develops clear guidelines for subordinates who then operate freely with no further direction unless they ask for help. However, the free-rein or "hands-off" AM does not abandon all control since the manager is ultimately accountable for the actions (or lack of actions) of workers. The free-rein AM delegates to a great extent in an effort to motivate the office workers to their fullest.

Based on what you have just read, answer the questions on the following page.

Respond to the following questions:

1. At this stage of your management development, which of the leadership styles best characterizes your total personality?

   _____

   _____

   _____

   _____

   _____

2. What are the strengths and weaknesses of the autocratic style?

   _____

   _____

   _____

   _____

   _____

3. What are the strengths and weaknesses of the participative style?

   _____

   _____

   _____

   _____

   _____

4. What do you look upon as the "best"—the ideal—leadership style? Why?

   _____

   _____

   _____

   _____

   _____

PROJECT 1-4: Case Study: Authority and the Substitute Administrative Office Manager

Before going on vacation from International Business Services, Ms. RosaLee Saikley asked Pat Belote, an administrative assistant, to assume the administrative manager's responsibilities in her absence. During the first day that Pat assumed the AM's responsibilities, she asked Samantha Stroba to undertake a specific task. Samantha's response was, "No way!" Rather than have a confrontation with her at the time, Pat asked Lawrence McFee, another administrative assistant, to do the task, which he willingly did.

Pat discussed this situation with Ms. Saikley on her return. Her reply was, "Although you have certain responsibilities during my absence, I am not transferring authority to you."

Respond to the following questions:

1. What are the implications of this situation to the direct line of authority for the AM?

_____

_____

_____

_____

2. In reviewing the entire delegating process, what do you think went wrong?

_____

_____

_____

_____

3. Upon the return of the AM, how might Ms. Saikley have responded more appropriately to Pat?

_____

_____

_____

_____

Write a one-page analysis of this situation, incorporating your answers to the questions. Be prepared to submit your paper or discuss it in class as directed by your instructor.

PROJECT 1-5: *The Experienced, But Scared, Administrative Manager*

You are a member of Professional Business Women, a professional organization that meets monthly during the lunch hour at a nearby hotel. Today, you are sitting next to Sadie McLaughlin, who is past president of the organization. You are pleased because you have admired her from afar for some time. You are sure you can learn something from her 20 years as an administrative manager.

Surprisingly, Sadie isn't in the best of moods and wants to "vent" over a situation that happened that morning in a meeting at work. Sadie shares with you that she is sure her job is in jeopardy. The president of Sadie's company has hired a consultant (as it turns out, from your company, International Business Services) to complete a comprehensive study of all positions at her company. The consultant will study technological work processes, reporting channels, salaries, and career paths in the organization. The study will take approximately three months to complete, according to the president, and all employees are asked to cooperate. The last thing the president said at the meeting was, "Expect some changes around here for the better!" Sadie is devastated. She apparently hasn't seen your name tag and doesn't know you are the administrative manager from International Business Services.

Respond to the following questions:

1. What is the central difficulty that Sadie is experiencing?

2. What is your role? Do you just listen or do you let her know how you are involved in this predicament?

3. If asked, what advice would you give Sadie?

As directed by your instructor, study the project information. Then, working with one of your classmates, role play the situation. Discuss with the classmate how you will respond to the conversation initiated during the luncheon. Your instructor may ask that you submit a team project based on your analysis.

INTERNET RESEARCH ASSIGNMENTS

PROJECT 1-6: *Investigating the Outlook for Administrative Support Occupations*

Each day administrative managers work with persons holding administrative support jobs. In this project, you will learn more about several administrative support jobs, the holders of which may report directly to the administrative manager or to an office supervisor, depending upon the size of the organization.

Workers in the administrative support group include those who prepare and keep records, operate office equipment; arrange schedules and make reservations; collect, distribute, or account for money, material, mail, or messages; or perform similar administrative duties. While administrative support jobs are located in virtually all industries, they are concentrated in the fast-growing service sector. Because of this concentration, the number of jobs is expected to grow rapidly.

Directions: Go to the course web site, **http://odgers.swlearning.com**, to locate the latest *Occupational Outlook Handbook*, located on the U.S. Department of Labor's web site, to learn about (1) the nature of the work; (2) working conditions; (3) employment; (4) training, other qualifications, and advancement; (5) job outlook; and (6) earnings for support jobs, such as the following:

Bank tellers

Bookkeeping, accounting, and auditing clerks

Customer service representatives

Computer equipment operators

Hotel and motel clerks

Receptionists

Word processors

Present your findings in a short oral or written report, as requested by your instructor.

PROJECT 1-7: *Administrative Management Resources on the Internet*

Situation: During your study of administrative management, you may be assigned case reports, research projects, or term papers for which research will be needed. The following journals and publications may aid you in locating references pertaining to the field of administrative management.

Directions: Locate the home pages of the journals on the Internet, retrieve file PRJ01-7 from the Data CD, and complete the form shown below by recording relevant information about each publication (audience, purpose of journal, how to subscribe, *etc.*).

Name of Journal	Type of Information Gained from Research (1–2 sentence(s))
Business Week	
Working Woman	
Inc	
OfficePro	
OfficeSolutions	

HANDS-ON COMPUTER ASSIGNMENTS

(Note: The hands-on computer assignments for each chapter in the Activity workbook are optional, depending on the level of computer knowledge students possess, the availability and type of equipment and software, and the preferences of the instructor.)

PROJECT 1-8: *Word Processing: Traditional vs. Current Workplace* *Values*

This activity is designed to measure your reaction to two examples of employee values that are in conflict. The traditional and current workplace values are contrasted in the examples.

Complete the following tasks:

1. Retrieve file PRJ01-8, which shows the following two scenarios, from the Data CD. Assume that office workers who report to you reflect these opinions. Contrast and react to each scenario in three sentences or less.

2. Use the software thesaurus as you compose and the spell checker as you edit your responses. Use your creativity to format this activity; apply each of the bold, underline, and italic features at least once.

SCENARIO A	
Traditional	Tomorrow will be just like today; I just need to hang in there till I can find an easier job.
Current	Nobody knows what tomorrow holds; constant learning is part of my job.

SCENARIO B	
Traditional	The more subordinates who report to me, the more important I am.
Current	I belong to a team; we fail or succeed together.

PROJECT 1-9: *Spreadsheet: Controlling Costs Using Spreadsheets*

This activity is designed to show how AMs use spreadsheets to control and assess costs and profits.

Complete the following tasks:

1. Retrieve file PRJ01-9 from the Data CD, which contains the profit worksheet as shown below. Enter correct formulas to calculate the gross profit per quarter and the totals for the revenue and expense columns. (Hint: Revenue less Expenses = Gross Profit)

2. Print a copy of the spreadsheet and a copy showing the formulas, as directed by your instructor.

Profit Worksheet For Fiscal Year			
Quarters	**Revenue**	**Expenses**	**Gross Profit**
1	$ 60,000	$ 22,000	
2	$ 55,000	$ 23,000	
3	$ 75,250	$ 30,050	
4	$ 89,000	$ 38,000	
Total			

CHAPTER 2
HANDLING ADMINISTRATIVE MANAGEMENT CHALLENGES

REVIEW ACTIVITY

PROJECT 2-1: *True-False and Fill in the Blanks*

Directions: Indicate your answer to each of the following statements by circling T or F in the Answers column.

Answers

1. E-mail has not played a role in any employment law cases to date.   T   F

2. You can simply delete an e-mail just like any file and it is essentially gone.   T   F

3. Information technology with its access to information has changed the way we work, play, and live.   T   F

4. When you are faced with an ethical dilemma, you should ask yourself: Is it legal? Is it balanced? Is it right?   T   F

5. Corporate culture is a very visible force that drives an organization.   T   F

6. Workers find it quite easy to balance work and family responsibilities today.   T   F

7. Information gathered via computer monitoring can be used by administrative managers to coach employees.   T   F

8. One way to organize your portfolio is according to projects you have completed, training you have had, and skills you can perform.   T   F

9. By joining professional organizations, you become an "outsider."   T   F

10. Certification is a way for employers to ensure a level of competency, skills, or quality in a particular area.   T   F

Directions: Fill in the blanks below in each statement with the correct responses.

1. _____ means what people think of the way you do business and how they assess your character as a businessperson.

2. The act of continuing steadfastly and being committed is _____.

3. A person's _____ is his or her broad view of an event.

4. The goal of workers to balance responsibilities on the job with responsibilities at home can be defined as _____ _____.

5. Reasons for monitoring workers' activities are usually defined in a _____ _____.

PRACTICAL EXPERIENCE ASSIGNMENTS

PROJECT 2-2: *Field Research: Evaluating New Work Arrangements*

In undertaking this field research project, you will talk with an administrative manager and one or more office workers who are employed by a firm that has broken from the traditional 5-day, 40-hour workweek and established a different work schedule. It will be interesting to learn if any employees are sharing a job, telecommuting, or working on a permanent part-time schedule. When interviewing the employees, your objective will be to gain a sincere, frank appraisal of the overall effectiveness of the new work arrangements.

Directions: Using as a guide the questions contained in the table below, arrange for an interview with the office workers in a firm now operating under any new work schedule. Be sure to take complete notes on all impressions—good or bad—conveyed by the workers. When you make your written or oral report, you will want to present a comprehensive picture of how the office workers' lifestyle, productivity, and morale have been affected as a result of the company's conversion to these new arrangements.

Your instructor will provide you with information on the type of report you should prepare. If you are making an oral report, you may want to include a PowerPoint® presentation if the equipment and supplies are available.

Question	Response or Effect
1. Name of company and kind of business organization, product line, service rendered.	
2. Describe the type of new work schedule and the old work schedule from which the conversion was made.	
3. Number of workers under new work arrangement.	
4. Length of time employees have worked under new arrangement.	
5. Number of and nature of workers not covered by new work arrangement.	

Question	Response or Effect
6. If any employees are telecommuting, explain the nature of their work assignments and indicate the reactions of the workers and management to this kind of arrangement.	
7. Indicate any effects of the new work schedule on each of the following workplace factors: • Productivity • Tardiness/absenteeism • Worker tensions • Morale level • Cooperation among workers • Customer service • Supervision • Use of facilities & equipment	

Your instructor may ask you to obtain additional information other than that asked for in the chart above. If so, make a note of that information so that you can ask about it during the interviews. Be sure to include the additional information in your report.

PROJECT 2-3: E-Mail from the President: Important or Bothersome?

At International Business Services, the president is starting to e-mail little sayings each Monday morning to everyone on the corporate network system. The statement, "Something to think about. . . ." prefaces these sayings.

> This week's saying is "Small minds discuss people, ordinary minds discuss events, and great minds discuss ideas." Last week's saying was a quote by Edison that said, "I never did anything worth doing by accident, nor did any of my inventions come by accident; they came by work." At lunch, a group of employees are discussing the president's behavior. Some think it is inappropriate; most don't mind it and find it rather amusing or interesting. In other words, they read it and go about their business.

1. In your opinion, would receiving these sayings in this manner at work bother you?

   _____

   _____

   _____

   _____

   _____

2. Do employees have the right to criticize the president of an organization for his or her behavior? Explain.

   _____

   _____

   _____

   _____

   _____

3. What if one or more of the sayings are religious or have religious overtones? What would you suggest as an action for the employees?

   _____

   _____

   _____

   _____

   _____

PROJECT 2-4: *The Computer Monitoring Incident*

A consultant who specializes in computers at International Business Services recently shared the following situation about a call he made to the administrative offices of a large hotel in Phoenix.

> James Frederick, a customer relations representative at the hotel, was extremely upset. For the past month, the hotel he works for has been electronically monitoring his activities and performance by using a computer.
>
> He has just finished reading his computer-generated performance evaluation and takes exception to just about everything in the report. For example, he feels he was "written up" because, when he spoke with five customers about making reservations, the computer showed he forgot to mention promotion packages that could have improved his chances of getting the customers' booking. When James contacted the administrative manager about the report, she said that he misunderstood the purpose of computer monitoring. Its purpose, she explained, is to help employees do their jobs better. In fact, the AM said, that starting next month, prompts would appear on the computer screen to remind customer service representatives of promotions, along with the details of each promotion.

1. As a consultant, do you feel that the information just provided James would help him feel that computer monitoring is really intended to help him? Or do you think he may continue to be suspect of the hotel's motives?

   _____

   _____

   _____

2. In your opinion, what are some reasons James distrusts this new approach that is intended to "help" him?

   _____

   _____

   _____

Directions: Be prepared to review the case and discuss your opinions in a class discussion as requested by your instructor. Make any notes as reminders here.

_____

_____

_____

_____

_____

INTERNET RESEARCH ASSIGNMENT

PROJECT 2-5: Online Job Search Guide

Each day job hunters go online to see what jobs are available in their local area or nationally. The purpose of this assignment is to research some basic information about doing an online job search. Go to the Internet and enter search words such as *jobs*, *job search*, *finding a job*, *online job search*, *creating a resume*, or other search words that you can think of to locate information to the following questions:

• How do you protect your privacy when doing an online job search?

• How do you know that the web site does not share your information?

• How do you find jobs online?

• How do you create an Internet resume and post it for employers?

• What are some important reminders when doing an online job search?

Directions: Present your findings in a short oral or written report, as requested by your instructor. Use the space below to record the site information for each online job search address you found useful.

_____

_____

_____

_____

_____

_____

_____

_____

_____

_____

_____

_____

_____

HANDS-ON COMPUTER ASSIGNMENTS

PROJECT 2-6: Word Processing: Preparing a Resume to be Posted Online

This activity is designed to assist you in preparing a resume that could be posted online using Microsoft's Word Resume Wizard feature. To do this:

1. Under **File**, click **New**.

2. Locate the **Other Documents** folder tab, and select it. If your version of Word does not have an **Other Documents** folder tab, look in the **General Templates** folder tab. After you locate the **Other Documents** tab, select it.

3. In most versions of Word, the resume wizard will be an icon in the **Other Documents** tab folder.

4. Double-click **Resume Wizard**. If you don't see it, you may need to install it.

Complete the following tasks:

1. Begin Microsoft Word and open a new document using the Resume Wizard.

2. Answer all questions asked of you in the Wizard as you prepare an entry-level resume using the professional style format.

3. Select each placeholder in your wizard-generated resume and replace it with information of your own.

4. Print the document as requested by your instructor. Show your instructor your resume and ask for feedback on its form, content, and appearance. Make any necessary corrections; keep the resume for future use in your job search. You may find it a good idea to save your document on a disk so that you can make changes when your work experience or other areas listed on your resume change.

5. Research how to post a resume online and make notes as to the procedure for future reference. Enter search words such as *resume, online resume, job search,* or similar words or phrases to begin your Internet research. Report your research results to the class and ask for feedback from your classmates as directed by your instructor.

PROJECT 2-7: Spreadsheet: Calculating Severance Pay

This activity is designed to practice using formulas to calculate severance pay amounts for downsized workers.

Complete the following tasks:

1. Retrieve PRJ02-7 from the Data CD; this file contains the worksheet shown below.

2. Use formulas to calculate severance pay at 50% and 75% of the monthly salary for each of the following employees as shown below in the table.

3. Sort by Employee Identification number in ascending order. Using the AutoFormat feature, select an appropriate format of your choice and apply it to your spreadsheet. Your instructor may provide you with additional information as to the procedure for developing this spreadsheet. In addition you may be assigned to a team to prepare an analysis of the spreadsheet.

4. Print the information as requested by your instructor.

Name	ID#	Monthly Salary	Salary @ 50%	Salary @ 75%
John Ferkovich	948-54-3333	$1,999.00		
Leonard Seaborn	876-33-2456	$3,245.00		
Kenny Mangum	526-73-5433	$4,300.00		
Hope Bertone	529-87-5432	$4,321.00		
Brett Hamburg	768-78-6844	$2,300.00		
Bob Bailey	526-66-6844	$4,521.00		

CHAPTER 3

ADMINISTRATIVE MANAGEMENT ACTIVITIES IN THE WORKPLACE

REVIEW ACTIVITY

PROJECT 3-1: *Matching Terminology*

Directions: In the Answers column, write the letter of the item in Column 1 that is most often associated with each item in Column 2.

Column 1	Column 2	Answers
A. Information literacy	1. Seeing, thinking, and acting in culturally mindful ways	1. ____
B. Virtual coordinator (VC)	2. Process by which information and human attitudes are exchanged with others	2. ____
C. Ergonomics	3. Day-to-day literacy related to employability and skills required	3. ____
D. Global literate	4. Ability to use computers and technology to find, analyze, and use information	4. ____
E. Communication	5. A collection of computers and devices working together	5. ____
F. Anti-virus program	6. An applied science devoted to the workplace	6. ____
G. Network	7. A program to protect computers	7. ____
H. Internet	8. A natural extension of leadership	8. ____
I. Teambuilding	9. World's largest network system	9. ____
J. Workplace literacy	10. Someone who can adapt quickly, step in where needed, and access information	10. ____

PRACTICAL EXPERIENCE ASSIGNMENTS

PROJECT 3-2: Selecting a New Administrative Office Manager

As you complete this project dealing with the selection of an administrative office manager, you will be critically analyzing questions such as these:

1. What personal characteristics am I looking for?

2. How much of a salary increase over the applicant's present earnings must I offer to attract the job seeker?

3. How important is an advanced degree?

Here is some background information you will need in order to select the best applicant. (The personal information was volunteered by the candidates. It is illegal to ask candidates for specific ages, marital information, etc. as shown in Table 3-2.)

TOPS IN KAN Beef Products is located in a combined meat packing plant and office building in Kansas City, Missouri. The fourth floor of the building, sound proof and air-conditioned, is used for the administrative offices. All accounting, credit, and human resources work and office services are provided in one large office. A breakout of the present work force is shown in Table 3-1.

	Table 3-1 OFFICE PERSONNEL AT TOPS IN KAN		
Department or Service	Men	Women	Age Range (yrs)
Accounting and Business Services	6	2	24-45
Human Resources	1	2	30-50
Information Technology	4	10	20-55
Mailing, Copying, etc.	2	7	19-60

Bonnie Harrow, the present administrative manager, is 58 years old. She has been with the firm for 30 years but has decided to retire at the end of the month because of ill health. Although it is the company's policy to promote from within whenever vacancies occur, in this instance the company president has decided to select someone from outside the organization in order to rejuvenate and update the administrative office systems. The president feels that as a result of Harrow's long tenure, the office work has gotten in a "rut."

The starting salary of the new administrative manager will be $40,000. Harrow has been receiving an annual salary of $42,500. It is expected that the new office manager's salary will be increased to $44,000 within three to four years.

Applicants for the position have been narrowed down to three candidates. Table 3-2 summarizes the personal data obtained from the candidates' applications and other information volunteered during their interviews.

Table 3-2 Personal Data of Candidates for Administrative Manager Position			
Factor	**Rose Carrera**	**Michael Hun**	**Jeffrey Berg**
Age and Marital Status	35 yrs., divorced	36 yrs., single	41 yrs., married
Number of Dependents	1 child	no information given	wife and 2 children
Education	Two years at university evening school (administrative and human resources management)	College graduate, B.S.; accounting major, computer information systems minor	Community college AA degree; 3 yrs, college evening division (marketing, accounting, computer systems)
Experience	Administrative assistant to company president, 5 yrs; credit manager, 7 yrs to present	Junior accountant, 1 yr; administrative manager, textile office—10 employees, 4 yrs; employment agency, owner and manager, 8 yrs to present	Yeoman, U.S. Navy, 4 yrs; office manager, metal manufacturing, 4 yrs; payroll manager, fuel oil distributor—22 employees, 10 yrs to present
Annual Salary	$38,000	$41,000	$43,000
Professional Associations and Certifications	Microsoft Office Specialist Certificates in Excel, Word, Access, PowerPoint, and Outlook	American Management Association	International Association of Administrative Professionals
Reasons for Desiring Change	Well satisfied with present position; just "shopping around"	Plagued by problems of small business ownership; looking for greater long-term security and stability	No opportunity for advancement; personality conflict with CEO

Directions: The president of the company has asked you to help select the new administrative office manager by answering each of the following questions.

1. Which one of the three candidates do you recommend be employed? Why?

_____

_____

2. For what reasons have you rejected the two other candidates?

_____

_____

Prepare an analysis to incorporate the answers to the questions above. Your instructor will provide information as to the format expected for the analysis and how you will present the information—either as an oral report or as a written report to submit, or both.

PROJECT 3-3: Gap in Employment Record

As the Administrative Office Manager at International Business Services, you are screening a group of applicants to fill an entry-level "catch all" position that would include working in the mailroom, copying, and delivering items to and from offices. You have in front of you what you think is a very qualified application. There is only one thing, however, that doesn't quite feel right. The applicant has a gap in his employment record. He put a sticky note on his application stating that he decided to "bum out for a year or so and travel around Europe."

Respond to the following questions:

1. Should this gap in employment be of any consequence to the hiring decision? Explain your reasons.

_____

_____

_____

_____

2. If you are really pleased with everything except the one item, what might you do to clarify your misgivings about this applicant's employability?

_____

_____

_____

_____

Prepare a written summary of your opinions and decisions to be used in a class discussion. Your instructor will guide you as to the way the information will be presented in class.

PROJECT 3-4: Personal Assessment — Your Administrative Management Abilities

Situation: Assume you are applying for an administrative management position and feel the need to personally assess your potential success in such a position before an interview. Using the listing in the table below of the major activities administrative managers perform, assess your strengths and weaknesses and what you plan to do to bring each area up to par.

Directions: Retrieve file PRJ03-4 on your Data CD and complete the table shown below by recording your assessment.

Assessment Tool for Administrative Manager's Abilities			
Activity	**Strengths**	**Weaknesses**	**Improvement Plan**
Human Resources Management			
Leadership and Communication Skills			
Administrative Services Management			
Workplace Systems and Technology			

Be prepared to submit the information to your instructor for comments if requested. You may be asked to work in a team to discuss how these areas of weakness may be improved.

INTERNET RESEARCH ASSIGNMENT

PROJECT 3-5: *Finding Administrative Management Jobs on the Internet*

Situation: Search the Internet and locate at least two job announcements that provide recent data on administrative management positions relative to training/education needed, essential skills required, preferred qualifications, and opportunities for employment. You can use major corporations, your local newspaper published online, local businesses or schools or government agencies as sources in your search. Ask your instructor for suggestions if you can't locate any information on administrative management positions. Your instructor may allow you to substitute a local newspaper advertisement section instead of using the Internet.

Directions: Using file PRJ03-5 on your Data CD, write one or two sentences in response to the questions listed in the table below. Prepare a short report based on the information you located for submission if requested by the instructor.

Question	Job Announcement #1	Job Announcement #2
1. Type or name of company and job title being advertised		
2. What training or educational requirement is mentioned?		
3. What essential skills are required?		
4. What preferred qualifications are requested?		
5. Are starting salaries or compensation plans cited? If so, what are they?		
6. Would you apply for a job at this company? Why or why not?		

HANDS-ON COMPUTER ASSIGNMENTS

PROJECT 3-6: Word Processing: Recruitment Flier

This activity is designed to review in a creative way one method of recruiting administrative professionals within an organization.

Complete the following tasks:

Create an original flier that advertises a job opening for the vice president of administrative services at International Business Services. Supply data relative to qualifications, application close and position start dates, and salary in a table format. The flier should be a two-fold (or tri-fold) flier, with company logo, contact information, and any other information you think is needed.

Format the table by using centering, italics, and bold letters for appearance and clarity. Insert clip art that you feel is appropriate and place it centered in the upper half of the flier. Apply appropriate color if you have a color printer available. Print the flier. Proofread the copy carefully and make any necessary corrections. Then print the number of copies suggested by your instructor to use in your class discussion and presentation.

PROJECT 3-7: *Spreadsheet: Controlling Budget Amounts*

This activity is designed to show how administrative managers use spreadsheets to track actual and budgeted monthly amounts.

Complete the following tasks:

1. Retrieve PRJ03-7 from the Data CD, which contains the Monthly Expenditure worksheet below. Enter correct formulas to calculate the percentage of over and under actual amounts as well as the totals for each of those columns.

2. Ask your instructor for information as to how to prepare the formulas if you are unclear how to proceed.

3. Print a copy of the spreadsheet and a copy showing the cell formulas. Be prepared to discuss what you interpret from the budget figures. What does over/under mean?

Monthly Expenditures for July			
	Actual	**Budgeted**	**% Over/Under**
Rent	$ 450	$ 450	
Phone	60	45	
Electric	80	90	
Gas	79	65	
Car Payment	320	320	
Insurance	49	49	
Total			

CHAPTER 4
EMERGING ELEMENTS IMPACTING ADMINISTRATIVE MANAGEMENT PRACTICES

REVIEW ACTIVITY

PROJECT 4-1: True-False and Fill in the Blanks

Directions: Indicate your answer to each of the following statements by circling T or F in the Answers Column.

Answers

1. Computer users addicted to the Internet are said to have computer addiction.

T F

2. It has been predicted that voice-recognition software programs will soon make keyboards obsolete.

T F

3. Managers need to be prepared to manage solutions rather than manage challenges.

T F

4. Change can cause workers to be fatigued and/or irritable.

T F

5. A paradigm is defined as a set of assumptions or a frame of reference.

T F

6. E-commerce is a financial transaction that occurs over an electronic network.

T F

7. Fortunately, entrenched bureaucracies do not exist today.

T F

8. Change management involves managing the changes organizations are experiencing.

T F

9. The first phase that workers experience when dealing with change is confrontation.

T F

10. Examples of noncore functions are security, information technology, and human resources.

T F

Directions: Complete the statements below by filling in the blanks with the correct phrase or word.

1. _____ _____ occurs when the computer consumes someone's entire social life.

2. _____ refers to looking for evidence of a more positive, less catastrophic, view of some change.

3. A set of practices designed to authorize, drive, and enable day-to-day decision-making at lower levels within an organization is known as _____.

4. The _____ _____ condenses the hours worked each week into fewer days.

5. _____ is a management strategy that utilizes service providers to perform noncore functions.

PRACTICAL EXPERIENCE ASSIGNMENTS

PROJECT 4-2: *Preparing an Organizational Chart of the Administrative Office Management Function*

You have just accepted the position of administrative office manager of the Gerardi Company, which has 120 office employees. The company is planning to centralize as many administrative services as possible and develop a staff department whose assignment will be to study and improve administrative systems. In addition, it is your plan to organize the work so that it will be properly supervised and controlled. As administrative office manager in charge of all administrative services, you report to the treasurer of the company, who in turn reports directly to the president.

The proposed plan of supervision includes the following personnel: (The estimated number of employees needed in each department, including the supervisor or the officer of that department, is given in parentheses.)

a) Mary Jo Carman, assistant administrative office manager, handles space management, office machines and equipment, and reports. (19)

b) Pamela H. Wong, chief accountant, is responsible for general accounting and budgeting. (15)

c) Glenn T. Sinatra, assistant human resources manager, handles factory personnel problems. Sinatra reports to the director of human resources, Janice D. Mangine, who, in her staff position, reports directly to the president. (12)

d) Lucy Key Crespin, assistant to the president, handles all legal affairs. (4)

e) Frederick M. McKnight is responsible for administrative systems, a staff position. (4)

f) Carolyn Healey-Bacon is in charge of internal auditing, a staff position. She has the title of auditor. (5)

g) Cynthia R. Corturillo, supervisor, directs the help desk operations. (15)

h) Patrick N. Shoemaker, supervisor, directs the records management department and mailing center. (10)

i) Mark D. Cervini, supervisor of office communications, is responsible for the telecommunications, reprographics, and micrographics. (20)

Directions: On the basis of the preceding information, prepare an organizational chart (either on the computer or by hand) showing the organization of the Gerardi Company. On the chart below each person's title, place the name of the person responsible for the direction or supervision of the work. Under each supervisor's name, indicate some of the typical activities that would be directed by that person.

Prepare a PowerPoint presentation of your chart if the equipment is available. Be prepared to discuss your chart with a team assigned by your instructor. Then, present your chart and defend your analysis as a team. Make a preliminary drawing of your chart in the space below.

PROJECT 4-3: *Computer Addiction in the Workplace*

RosaLee Saikley, administrative manager, has just had a conversation with several of the consultants at International Business Services. The consultants are upset because two of their administrative assistants are not doing their jobs. Specifically, they report that Pat Belote and Greg Kerr are receiving increasingly more complaints from customers. Customers state that Pat and Greg haven't followed through on commitments and are not available to handle calls directly. Instead, customers are being channeled to voice mail and forced to leave messages. Further, when any of the consultants go to their work areas, Pat and Greg are on the computer surfing sites on the Internet or in chat rooms writing responses. These actions appear to be non work-related.

Apparently Pat has recently told Ms. Saikley that she is going through a rough and upsetting time right now because she is in the process of getting a divorce and may lose custody of her two children to her husband. Rumor has it that Pat has become addicted to the Internet and spends up to 10 or more hours a day in chat rooms, instant messaging strangers, etc. when she should be taking care of her two young sons.

Respond to the following questions:

1. Is this issue that Pat has work-related or totally a personal one? If it is work-related, what steps are appropriate for Ms. Saikley to take at this moment? What is the plan of action if it is a personal issue?

_____

_____

_____

_____

_____

2. Over the next 10 years, do you believe computer addiction or Internet addiction disorder will be a serious issue in the workplace or will flexible work relationships negate or conceal the effects?

_____

_____

_____

_____

Prepare a brief outline of a report and ask your teacher to review it and make comments. Then prepare a short presentation you would make to a business group about Internet addiction.

PROJECT 4-4: Using Teams to Deal with Workplace Changes

In most matters at International Business Services, Ms. Gibson prefers to use a work team to deal with problems or issues when they arise rather than to bring in outside consultants. Consistent with this philosophy, she has asked you (RosaLee Saikley, AOM) to facilitate a work team that is charged with the responsibility of developing an in-house seminar for employees who wish to be able to adapt to change more efficiently.

Respond to the following questions:

1. How would you proceed in developing this seminar? For example, would you meet formally or informally with the other members? Where? When? How long?

    _____

    _____

    _____

    _____

    _____

2. Rather than an in-house seminar, are there other forums available to help colleagues adapt to change?

    _____

    _____

    _____

    _____

    _____

3. What topics or areas should be included in this training?

    _____

    _____

    _____

    _____

    _____

Prepare a short report to submit to your instructor as requested. Be prepared to participate in a group discussion as directed by your instructor.

INTERNET RESEARCH ASSIGNMENT

PROJECT 4-5: Current Workplace Trends

The workplace is undergoing changes on a daily basis. The purpose of this activity is for you to update your knowledge of workplace trends by visiting the web site for the course at **http://odgers.swlearning.com** to locate links to determine current workplace trends. Click on these links to learn about various trends. Or you can simply enter workplace trends or other search words to find sites on your own. *The Futurist* magazine, published by the World Future Society, may also give you additional information if you access its web site.

Directions: Present your findings in a short oral or written report, as requested by your instructor. Use the space below to make notes from your searches and to develop an outline for your report.

_____

_____

_____

_____

_____

_____

_____

_____

_____

_____

_____

_____

_____

_____

_____

_____

_____

HANDS-ON COMPUTER ASSIGNMENTS

PROJECT 4-6: Word Processing: Creating Organizational Charts

This activity is designed for you to practice creating different organizational charts on the computer using the word processing diagram gallery window from the drawing toolbar.

Complete the following tasks:

1. Locate the organizational chart for International Business Services that appears in the front of your activity workbook, or an alternative such as an organizational chart of your school or from your employer. Using that organizational chart, format it in two different ways.

2. The two formatted organizational charts should be designed using the a) traditional hierarchical organizational chart that is required, and b) the cycle diagram or the target design.

3. Proofread your charts. Print a copy of your charts and present them to your instructor as requested. You may be required to present the charts to the class and to participate in a group discussion led by your instructor or a team leader. You may want to do research in the library or on the Internet in which you search for organizational charts in management textbooks or in articles about organizational charts. Review the section in your text to refresh your memory on the purposes of organizational charts.

Use the space below to draw a preliminary organizational chart in the traditional hierarchical format to give you an idea how the chart shows positions and relationships.

PROJECT 4-7: Spreadsheet: Charting Comparison Data

This activity is designed to show how administrative managers use spreadsheets and to create a simple 3-D column chart to compare survey data.

Complete the following tasks:

1. Retrieve file PRJ04-7 from the Data CD, which contains the survey data worksheet on workplace trends as shown here.

2. Plot a comparison of the three industries in a 3-D column chart using appropriate titles for the chart and x-axis. Show the legend (what each block stands for using color if possible) beneath the chart title. Your instructor may need to give you guidance on the preparation of this spreadsheet to prepare a 3-D column chart.

3. Print a copy of the 3-D column chart only. Your instructor will evaluate your draft and offer suggestions for improvement. Make any changes necessary; then print a copy for submission to your instructor as requested.

Trend	Legal	Medical	Insurance
Empowerment	102	77	82
Teams	35	88	65
Horizontal Organizations	73	65	59

CHAPTER 5

MANAGING INFORMATION, TECHNOLOGY, AND TRAINING IN THE WORKPLACE

REVIEW ACTIVITY

PROJECT 5-1: Matching Terminology

Directions: In the Answers column, write the letter of the item in Column 1 that is most often associated with each item in Column 2.

Column 1	Column 2	Answers
A. System	1. Telephone lines, cable, cellular, radio, and satellites	1. ____
B. Computer system	2. Collaborative network	2. ____
C. Portable skills	3. Centralized entity responsible for all training and education at a given company	3. ____
D. Workplace literacy	4. A group of parts interrelated to form a unified whole to work together	4. ____
E. Communication media	5. A group of computer devices connected, coordinated, and linked to work as one	5. ____
F. Virtual organizations	6. Possession of skills you can transfer from what you know to slightly new situations	6. ____
G. Virtual assistant	7. A way a person learns at his or her own pace using computers and telecommunication devices	7. ____
H. Corporate university	8. Ability to use words clearly and communicate with brevity and accuracy in context of a given job	8. ____
I. E-learning	9. Aid to making a task easier with equipment and procedures	9. ____
J. Technology	10. An independent entrepreneur who offers support business services in a virtual environment	10. ____

PRACTICAL EXPERIENCE ASSIGNMENTS

PROJECT 5-2: Observation Tour — Systems in Your Community

Your office management class is planning to take an "observation tour"—visiting legal, medical, and city government offices in your community. Since the main intent of these visits is to observe common systems in action, what type of guidelines should be in place before taking this visit?

Directions:

1. List several guidelines you might follow. You will want to address the following:

   Getting to the destinations—how travel will be provided, who is going to which offices, which offices have agreed to host your group, dress requirements, safety regulations, what will you be observing, and the like. You will be able to think of other guidelines to add to your list as you plan your visits.

   _____

   _____

   _____

   _____

   _____

   _____

   _____

   _____

2. As directed by your instructor, complete this tour and report back to your class your observations in a brief one- to two-page report. Prepare for an in-depth class discussion of your observations. Your instructor may ask you to submit a written report of your visits.

PROJECT 5-3: *Contract Training Programs Through Community Colleges*

You have been asked to meet with the contract training administrator at Rio Salado Community College in Phoenix to work out a training program specially designed for employees at International Business Services. The types of programs the college offers happen to be similar to those mentioned in Table 5.2 in your textbook. Answer the following questions and prepare a report to submit to your instructor as requested after your visit. Justify your listing of courses for training.

1. Before meeting with the community college administrator, what process would you go through to determine what the training needs are at International Business Services (e.g., survey, casual conversations, meetings, etc.)?

   _____

   _____

   _____

   _____

   _____

   _____

2. Which five topics, in order of priority, would you select and why?

   a. _____

   _____

   _____

   b. _____

   _____

   c. _____

   _____

   d. _____

   _____

   e. _____

   _____

Directions: Make a plan so that you can check off the tasks as they are completed. Be sure to make an appointment with the contract training administrator so that he or she will be aware of your visit and the types of information that you plan to discuss.

PROJECT 5-4: Upgrading Computer Systems

Five workstations need to be upgraded at International Business Services. You, as the administrative office manager, have been asked to determine the specifications before a meeting with Ms. Gibson next Wednesday.

1. How would you go about the task of determining what current products are on the market for a computer system?

_____

_____

_____

_____

2. Considering the type of work International Business Services office workers process, and that you have to stay within a $15,000 budget, what type of multimedia computer system would you recommend for the five workstations?

_____

_____

_____

_____

Directions: Report on your methods to find current products. Prepare a brief one-page report to submit to your instructor as directed. After you have reviewed the products, specify which system you would recommend and why.

INTERNET RESEARCH ASSIGNMENT

PROJECT 5-5: Computer Hardware Specifications Research

Situation: Locate the home pages of IBM, Dell, Gateway, and Compaq and determine the best computer system under $2,000 from each of the computer hardware companies. Since companies will, of course, list the features of their equipment, it may be your task to determine what is "best" from the features presented. Determine not only the best desktop system but also the best laptop/portable system. You may want to look for information from computer magazines, such as *PCWorld,* that periodically review various types of equipment and software. Making an appointment to interview a representative from one of the office equipment stores in your area may also give you a different viewpoint on what is considered ideal in purchasing types of equipment.

Directions: Using file PRJ05-5 on your Data CD, describe the computer system specifications for each company by using the form below. Print a copy of your report to submit to your instructor.

Computer Company	Description of Specifications Desktop System	Description of Specifications Laptop System
IBM		
Dell		
Gateway		
Compaq		
Based on your research, which company would you buy your computer systems from and why?		

HANDS-ON COMPUTER ASSIGNMENTS

PROJECT 5-6: Word Processing: Training Topics

This activity is designed to review the new training topics and to provide practice editing and formatting changes.

Complete the following tasks:

1. Retrieve PRJ05-6 from the Data CD; this file contains the information from the bulleted list in Table 5.2 in your textbook on page 118.

2. Edit the document in the following ways:

   • Perform a descending sort on the items.

   • Format the topics to the correct upper or lower case.

   • Change the dot bullet to a different image (bullet, picture) of your choice.

   • Key the list in a 3-column format.

3. Print a copy of the results to submit to your instructor. Be prepared to discuss the information as directed.

PROJECT 5-7: Spreadsheet: Forecasting Sales by Using a Line Chart

This activity is designed to allow you to practice creating a worksheet which forecasts this year's sales based on last year's sales figures.

Complete the following tasks:

1. Retrieve PRJ05-7 from the Data CD; this file contains the worksheet shown below. In Column 3, enter formulas based on a 15 percent increase projection for this year's sales over last year's sales. Review the procedures for this type of calculation with your instructor to be sure you understand how to proceed. Show the increase in sales amount in column 4.

2. Print a line chart showing the trends between last year's and this year's sales figures. Use appropriate titles, legend placement, and grids of your choice to enhance its appearance and meaning. Review your document with your instructor for feedback. Make any necessary corrections.

3. Print a copy of the worksheet and line graph to submit to your instructor.

SALES FORECAST			
Product	**Sales Last Year**	**Projected Sales**	**Increase in Sales**
Printer Paper	$ 435,000		
Toner	$ 225,100		
CD-RWs	$ 98,473		

CHAPTER 6
STAFFING PRACTICES: EMPLOYMENT LAWS AND JOB ANALYSIS

REVIEW ACTIVITY

PROJECT 6-1: Fill in the Blanks

Directions: Complete the sentences below by filling in the blanks with the correct word or phrase.

1. The _____ _____ _____ ___ _____ prohibits discrimination on the basis of sex in the payment of wages or benefits, where the work is similar in skill, effort, and responsibility for the same employer under similar conditions.

2. The agency tasked to oversee compliance with the Civil Rights Act is the _____ _____ _____ _____.

3. An _____ is a court order requiring a person or corporation to do or not to do a particular act.

4. Title VII was amended in 1972 and became known as the _____ _____ _____ Act.

5. To protect pregnant women from discrimination in the workplace, the _____ _____ _____ was passed.

6. Unwelcome sexual advances, requests for sexual favors, and other verbal or physical conduct of a sexual nature, or creating a hostile workplace are known as _____ _____.

7. *Quid pro quo* means _____ _____ _____.

8. The _____ _____ _____ _____ is considered one of the most important antidiscrimination laws passed since 1964.

9. In _____ an impartial third party tries to bring sides in a disagreement into common agreement.

10. An action requiring significant difficulty or expense for an employer is known as _____ _____.

11. Eligible employees can take up to 12 weeks of unpaid, job-protected leave in a 12-month period for specified family and medical reasons under the _____ and _____ _____ _____.

12. _____ _____ may be available to pay for actual monetary loss, for future monetary losses, and for mental anguish and inconvenience where intentional discrimination is found against an employer.

13. If an employer acted with malice or reckless indifference in discriminating against employees, _____ _____ may be available.

PRACTICAL EXPERIENCE ASSIGNMENTS

PROJECT 6-2: Evaluating a Job Description

As an experiment, you as the administrative manager want to see how well your workers can prepare their own job descriptions. Debra Rosales, your company's receptionist, has given you the following version of her job. What is wrong with her job description?

Directions: Try your hand at rewriting the job description to reflect the improvements you recommend. Prepare your revision for submission to your instructor as directed. You may use the form below or prepare a similar one that you believe does the job and shows the descriptions correctly.

Job Description	May 23, 200-
Debra Rosales Job: Receptionist 1	

General Duties:

1. Under the direction of Bob Tice, the Assistant Manager of H.R., I place, receive, and route phone calls.

2. Also, I do the following

   - Provide general information to callers or visitors.
   - Greet and direct visitors.
   - Provide telephone directory assistance
   - Take telephone messages.

3. Sometimes I help out by sorting and opening incoming mail but I don't deliver it.

4. And I often have to use the fax machine and the copier. I am being trained to learn electronic mail on the PC and will start doing this work in a few weeks.

5. I do whatever other work Mr. Tice assigns me.

Qualifications:

1. I must communicate clearly and accurately.

2. I need to know our company's mailing and shipping procedures.

3. I must use the phone system to receive and transfer calls.

4. I try to be patient and courteous when working with people.

5. I had to have a high school diploma to get this job.

Write a brief report in which you analyze the description that Rosales prepared; then describe why your job description corrects any errors in the original.

PROJECT 6-3: The Physically Challenged Office Worker

When Karol Newton was 17 years old, she was in a serious motorcycle accident that required the amputation of her right leg. She was fitted with an artificial prosthesis that enables her to function nearly as well as anyone under most circumstances. She is currently 25 years old and is the mother of an active 3-year-old son.

Karol, a high school graduate, learned from a friend six months ago that there was a department of rehabilitation near her home where she could obtain assistance and training designed to aid her in preparing for a career position as an office worker. She was hired by International Business Services last month as a receptionist trainee and was hoping that her coworkers would treat her as they would any other worker. Unfortunately, three of her coworkers continually refuse to let her carry papers dropped off by clients to the various offices; they instead periodically pick up any papers from the delivery in-basket and distribute them for her.

Karol is concerned that she is being treated as though she is helpless or "different." She has started getting into conflict situations with other employees regarding topics on issues that do not relate to her physical condition. She has come to you, the AM, and has told you she is thinking about leaving her job.

Answer the following questions.

1. What do you feel is the major problem in this case?

_____

_____

_____

_____

_____

_____

2. How will you handle the situation at this point?

_____

_____

_____

_____

_____

Be prepared to discuss this situation in class. Your instructor may ask that you prepare an outline of your analysis of the case for the discussion and/or to submit.

PROJECT 6-4: Studying the Job Descriptions of Coworkers

In the computer center of Lakeland Inc. the supervisor of computer operations, Teresa Savage, has become aware of a serious morale problem. She believes that much of the problem stems from her workers who are more concerned with their own individual jobs than the overall well-being of the company. For example, this past week she has sensed a conflict among her data-entry operators who appear to be working in isolation. They only try to meet their own individual goals and are completely unconcerned about the direction in which the firm plans to head. These are the same workers who appear very insensitive to the priorities that were established by the systems analysts and programmers.

Savage believes her people must learn to pull together as a team and become more aware of the firm's perspectives about its future. While she was exploring her concerns with her boss, Bruce York, he broke in to say:

> I see where you are coming from, Teresa. What we've got to do is convince these people that they're partners in our company. I've got an idea. Let's give each of your people a copy of all the job descriptions for everyone working in the center—the analysts, programmers, computer operators, data-entry operations, and yes, my job description and yours. Ask them to study all the job descriptions for the next several days and then let's set up a meeting with them. At that meeting, here is what I would like us to do . . . .

Directions: Prepare a list of the direct questions you would ask your workers explaining how their study of the job descriptions can lead to a team orientation. What outcomes do you expect the meeting to provide that will enable you to start cultivating a climate in which the workers feel like partners?

_____

_____

_____

_____

_____

_____

_____

_____

_____

_____

Prepare an analysis of this case. Be ready to discuss the case in class as directed by your instructor.

INTERNET RESEARCH ASSIGNMENT

PROJECT 6-5: Equal Employment Opportunity Commission Cases

The EEOC is continually reviewing discrimination cases from workers in organizations governed by U.S. employment laws. Go to the web site **http://eeoc.gov/** or search various newspapers and read at least three current cases that the EEOC has recently reviewed. In particular, ask yourself as you read each case:

• What is the primary discrimination issue that the case is based upon?

• How did the EEOC rule in each case?

• What is your opinion as to the verdict or decision reached in each case? In other words, was it fair and impartial and based on the pronouncements of the law?

Present your findings in a short oral or written report, as requested by your instructor as follows:

Case # 1   Name(s) of people involved in the case:

_____

_____

_____

Discrimination factor claimed:

_____

_____

_____

Disposition of the case (what happened):

_____

_____

_____

Opinion of the verdict:

_____

_____

_____

Do a similar format for each case you review.

HANDS-ON COMPUTER ASSIGNMENTS

PROJECT 6-6: Word Processing: How to File an EEO Complaint

This activity is designed to assist you in understanding how discrimination complaints can be filed with the EEOC.

Complete the following tasks:

1. Retrieve PRJ06-6 from the Data CD; this file contains the document shown below. Read the information before you begin formatting it to get an idea of the types of information contained in this document.

2. Then, using the tables feature in your word processing software, re-format the information so that it is more understandable in table format. Use your creativity.

3. Print the table as requested by your instructor.

Filing a Charge

If you believe you have been discriminated against by an employer, labor union or employment agency when applying for a job or while on the job because of your race, color, sex, religion, national origin, age, or disability, or believe that you have been discriminated against because of opposing a prohibited practice or participating in an equal employment opportunity matter, you may file a charge of discrimination with the U.S. Equal Employment Opportunity Commission (EEOC).

Charges may be filed in person, by mail or by telephone by contacting the nearest EEOC office. If there is not an EEOC office in the immediate area, call toll free 800-669-4000 or 800-669-6820 (TDD) for more information. To avoid delay, call or write beforehand if you need special assistance, such as an interpreter, to file a charge.

There are strict time frames in which charges of employment discrimination must be filed. To preserve the ability of EEOC to act on your behalf and to protect your right to file a private lawsuit, should you ultimately need to, adhere to the following guidelines when filing a charge.

Title VII of the Civil Rights Act (Title VII) – Charges must be filed with EEOC within 180 days of the alleged discriminatory act. However, in states or localities where there is an anti-discrimination law and an agency authorized to grant or seek relief, a charge must be presented to that state or local agency. Furthermore, in such jurisdictions, you may file charges with EEOC within 300 days of the discriminatory act, or 30 days after receiving notice that the state or local agency has terminated its processing of the charge, whichever is earlier. It is best to contact EEOC promptly when discrimination is suspected. When charges or complaints are filed beyond these time frames, you may not be able to obtain any remedy.

AMERICANS WITH DISABILITIES ACT (ADA) – THE TIME REQUIREMENTS FOR FILING A CHARGE ARE THE SAME AS THOSE FOR TITLE VII CHARGES.

Age Discrimination in Employment Act (ADEA) – The time requirements for filing a charge are the same as those for Title VII and the ADA.

Equal Pay Act (EPA) - Individuals are not required to file an EPA charge with EEOC before filing a private lawsuit. However, charges may be filed with EEOC and some cases of wage discrimination also may be violations of Title VII. If an EPA charge is filed with EEOC, the procedure for filing is the same as for charges brought under Title VII. However, the time limits for filing in court are different under the EPA, thus, it is advisable to file a charge as soon as you become aware the EPA may have been violated.

PROJECT 6-7: Spreadsheet: Allocation of Time to Job Responsibilities

This activity is designed to provide practice using formulas to calculate percentage of time worked according to job responsibilities. You may use a spreadsheet format in your software program or do the calculations on a calculator and provide the information in a table or chart.

Complete the following tasks.

1. Retrieve PRJ06-7 from the Data CD; this file contains the worksheet shown below.

2. Format Hours/day in Task to two decimal positions.

3. Calculate the percentage of time spent using an absolute reference in your formula (i.e., C3). Format in percentage to two decimal positions. Copy the formula as needed.

4. Print the tables as requested by your instructor.

Breakout of Job Responsibilities for Administrative Assistant		
Task	**Hours/Day in Task**	**% of Time Spent**
Answering Phones	1.5	
Greeting Customers	1.0	
Creating Documents	1.5	
Calendaring Activities	0.75	
Taking and Transcribing Minutes	2.0	
Other Duties, as assigned	0.75	
Total Hours	7.5	

Review the total hours worked by an administrative assistant. Analyze the data and make recommendations for more efficient use of the assistant's time. Is there any time allocated for lunch, breaks, or personal time? What do you think of the time spent by an assistant? Write a report in which you address the time allocations and your recommendations to accompany the charts you printed.

CHAPTER 7

ON-THE-JOB EMPLOYEE PRACTICES

REVIEW ACTIVITY

PROJECT 7-1: Matching Terminology

Directions: In the Answers column, write the letter of the item in Column 1 that is most often associated with each item in Column 2.

Column 1	Column 2	Answers
A. Employment application form	1. Process of generating a pool of qualified applicants	1. ____
B. Orientation	2. Document that identifies the position and related information to perform the duties	2. ____
C. Performance appraisals	3. Process of choosing individuals who have relevant qualifications to fill jobs	3. ____
D. Employee recruitment	4. Form an applicant completes to be considered for a position	4. ____
E. Turnover	5. Process conducted to be sure applicants have the minimum requirements for the job	5. ____
F. Position approval form	6. Meeting or formal activity to prepare employees for working in a particular place	6. ____
G. Employee selection	7. Process of matching a new employee with an experienced one	7. ____
H. Structured, situational, or behavioral	8. Formal evaluation of employees by their supervisor, usually annually	8. ____
I. Buddy system	9. When workers leave their jobs	9. ____
J. Preliminary screening	10. Types of interviews	10. ____

PRACTICAL EXPERIENCE ASSIGNMENTS

PROJECT 7-2: Adapting Training Programs

Don Tinsley, administrative manager at Berlin Imports, asks you how he can adapt his training program to better serve the new employees he is seeing: the older worker, the advanced computer technology worker, the illiterate worker, the foreign-born worker.

Respond to the following questions:

1. What advice can you offer Tinsley after you research these issues?

2. To what extent does familiarization with computers and a person's educational level shape the design of a training program?

Research these work force challenges on the Internet or interview several human resources managers to get their input on how training should be developed to meet the needs of the changing work force.

Be ready to share your ideas as directed by your instructor for a group session. Make notes to keep your ideas clearly in mind.

PROJECT 7-3: Too Many Performance Appraisals to Do

Sandy Williams is reviewing her calendar and realizes that six-month reviews are coming up in three weeks. As usual, finding the time to do them is going to be a problem. With ten or more people to review, and a separate form to fill out and a separate file to update for each, she estimates that the process will take a minimum of 10 hours to complete. Where will she get that much time, she wonders. Sandy decides that one option is to limit the interviews to 15 minutes each. But she really doesn't feel right about doing that.

Respond to the following questions:

1. What do you think about the one option so far? Is it a viable option?

_____

_____

_____

_____

_____

_____

_____

_____

2. What other methods might Sandy use to get the job done in the best way, given her time constraints?

_____

_____

_____

_____

_____

_____

_____

_____

Research performance appraisals on the Internet and/or in the library. Your instructor may have management textbooks that can shed some light on the purpose of performance appraisals. Management and supervision textbooks usually discuss performance appraisals in-depth. You may use performance appraisals as key words in addition to the phrase performance evaluation to help you in your search. Write a brief analysis of your findings to use in a class discussion led by your instructor.

PROJECT 7-4: Job Performance Test

Mr. Chang has asked you to work with Ms. Black and Ms. Rodriguez to draft a performance test that will be administered to candidates who apply for the executive secretary opening for the sales manager. Within the first five minutes of your meeting, there appears to be a difference of opinion among the three of you, making it impossible for you to reach consensus.

Ms. Black wants to make this a one-hour, rigorous test; Ms. Rodriguez, on the other hand, wants to make it relatively simple and short in duration; you feel it should be somewhere in between the two suggestions. Your schedules only permit you to meet today for 45 minutes and again next week for 30 minutes before you have to submit your final draft to Mr. Chang.

Respond to the following questions:

1. You feel you are the best one to bring the group together because of your neutral approach. How would you decide what to do to reach a consensus?

_____

_____

_____

_____

_____

_____

_____

2. Describe the type of performance test that, in your opinion, would be best for a candidate to take for this top position.

_____

_____

_____

_____

_____

_____

Prepare a short analysis of your ideas. Then develop an outline that includes the topics to be tested. Include the timing and any directions or equipment/supplies to be provided for the candidates. A group discussion will be led by your instructor.

INTERNET RESEARCH ASSIGNMENTS

PROJECT 7-5: Recent Decisions on Employment Discrimination

Situation: You are preparing for a class panel discussion on recent laws passed or amended dealing with employment discrimination. There are numerous web sites for this purpose. Search the Internet to locate web sites that update on a regular basis the most recent decisions on employment discrimination from not only the U.S. Supreme Court, but also the U.S. Circuit Courts of Appeal and others. The Equal Employment Opportunity Commission may be a search phrase that can lead you to various cases that have come before the EEOC. As you find useful sites, include them in the list for the discussion. Submit your list to the instructor as directed. Be prepared to discuss your findings in class.

Directions: Using file PRJ07-5 on your Data CD, list three items from your research dealing with recent decisions on employment discrimination; use the form below.

Case Name and Legal Body	Brief Description of Employment Discrimination Decision
1.	
2.	
3.	

HANDS-ON COMPUTER ASSIGNMENTS

PROJECT 7-6: *Word Processing: Writing a Help-Wanted Advertisement*

As a result of the growth in sales for the Crockett Company, you find it necessary to employ an assistant who will aid you by shouldering some of the office responsibility—copying, keyboarding, database management, and computerized calendaring. The software packages you use are primarily the latest versions of Microsoft Office Professional. As you reflect on the kind of person you seek, these thoughts run though your mind:

"I want a young person, age 25 through 30, someone who is 'with it' and 'has his or her head on straight.' I don't want an old-timer who is too set in his or her ways. But, of course, I do want experience—at least two years of supervisory work in office services."

"I can probably work best with someone of my sex, but I won't get uptight about that point—I'm looking for a qualified assistant, not for a male or a female. Someone told me— I don't recall who—to steer away from divorced people, for they are not dependable or stable."

"Looking around our offices, I see that we have few workers from any of the minority groups—guess I had better make a big push to bring in a minority worker. Let's see, my budget for next year will allow me to offer $30,500 to the right person."

Complete the following tasks:

1. While at the computer, compose and print a help-wanted advertisement for this position.

2. Make the advertisement one that will excite interest and spark the imagination of the very person you want to hire.

3. Make sure that your completed advertisement complies with the law and in no way will result in a complaint from the local EEOC.

Prepare your advertisement and be ready to participate in a discussion with several members of your class in which you compare the components of your advertisements. Would any one of the advertisements cause a problem with compliance with an employment law? Defend your case.

Use the space below to draft some features or criteria that you want to be sure to include in the advertisement.

PROJECT 7-7: Word Processing: Training Survey

This activity is designed to determine the extent to which training is given in organizations in your community.

Complete the following tasks:

1. Retrieve PRJ07-7 from the Data CD; this file contains the table shown below.

2. Interview three individuals who have worked at a job for at least six months. Ask them the questions in the table to determine if they have received training in their current positions. Add some details about that training.

3. Print the table.

4. Be prepared to share your interview results with the class as directed by your instructor.

Questions	Person #1 Responses	Person #2 Responses	Person #3 Responses
1. What type of training do you receive through your current employer?			
2. Do you pay for this training yourself or does your employer?			
3. In what ways could your current employer better prepare you for your job?			

PROJECT 7-8: Spreadsheet: Trends in Recruitment of Employees

This activity is designed to enable you to create a simple bar chart, given worksheet data.

Complete the following tasks:

1. Retrieve PRJ07-8 from the Data CD; this file contains the worksheet shown below.

2. Construct and print a bar chart showing a comparison of trends in the recruitment of employees. Use appropriate titles, legends, and labels to enhance its appearance and meaning.

Sources	Year 1	Year 2	Year 3
Online Applications	55	144	212
Newspaper Ads	100	75	80
Walk-Ins	150	125	90

CHAPTER 8
EMPLOYEE COMPENSATION, RECOGNITION, AND COMPANY POLICIES

REVIEW ACTIVITY

PROJECT 8-1: Fill in the Blanks.

Directions: Complete the sentences below by filling in the blanks with the correct word or phrase.

1. An unsolicited e-mail message that is sent to many recipients on a particular topic is known as _____ mail.

2. The Fair Labor Standards Act classifies employees as _____ or _____ employees.

3. _____ employees are usually not paid overtime.

4. The portion of an employee's pay that includes the whole array of benefits is _____ _____.

5. _____ _____ is based on established criteria, usually reflected in the employee's performance appraisal.

6. Unemployment compensation may also be called _____ _____ and provides unemployed workers with benefits.

7. When an employee has a death in the immediate family, he or she can ask for _____ _____.

8. Retirement benefits established and funded by employees and employers are _____ _____.

9. A _____ is an authoritative directive for conduct.

10. Materials that communicate company policies to workers are commonly called _____ _____.

11. A request for an employee to leave his or her job involuntarily is a _____.

12. In some states, employers can fire an employee for no reason or any reason if the state has _____ _____.

13. Associations of employees to represent work force concerns and interests during negotiation with management are _____ _____.

14. Most union contracts provide for a _____ _____, whereby the employees and union can air their issues in a formal procedure.

15. The law that governs minimum wage rates, limits the weekly hours employees work through overtime provisions, and discourages oppressive child labor is the _____ _____ _____ _____ ____ _____.

PRACTICAL EXPERIENCE ASSIGNMENTS

CASE STUDY 8-2: Establishing an Educational Assistance Program

To meet the needs of its growing work force and to further develop the skills and knowledge of its workers, LeBlanc Inc. has decided to establish an educational assistance program, effective in the fall of this year. You, the administrative manager of the firm, plus four supervisors, two office workers, and two plant workers have been selected as the task force team to plan the establishment and administration of such a program.

Directions: By answering each of the questions below, you will help make a contribution as a member of the task force.

1. Present a workable definition of the educational assistance plan at LeBlanc Inc.,
    — a definition that will be easily and clearly understood by all workers.

    _____

    _____

2. Should the plan be uniformly applied throughout all departments and divisions of the company? Explain.

    _____

    _____

3. Who will be responsible for administering the educational assistance program?

    _____

    _____

    _____

4. Who will be eligible to participate in the program? Should eligibility be restricted? In what respect?

    _____

    _____

5. Should the program require or allow an employee to register as a full-time student and carry a full-course load? Explain.

    _____

    _____

6. What kinds of schools should employees be allowed to attend?

    _____

    _____

    _____

7. Should employees be permitted to take any course they want, or must the courses be job related, or at least applicable to a degree that will help employees in their jobs?

_____

_____

_____

8. Should any limit be placed on the number of, or the dollar value of, courses that a worker may take during the school year? If so, what are your recommendations?

_____

_____

9. What costs should the educational assistance plan cover? Registration? Tuition? Books? Test fees? Lab fees? Application fees? Transportation? Graduation fees?

_____

_____

10. How can the educational assistance program be maintained so that it is used correctly and achieves the objectives for which it was designed?

_____

_____

11. Should the amount of reimbursement depend upon the grade received by the employee? If so, spell out your recommended reimbursement plan.

_____

_____

12. What will be your "sales promotion pitch" to your employees to explain why the company is offering this new employee benefit? Incidentally, the program will cost your firm about $2.05 per week per employee who participates. How will you encourage employees to participate in the program?

_____

_____

13. How will LeBlanc Inc. be able to determine if the educational assistance plan is benefiting the company? Develop a set of criteria to be used in evaluating the effectiveness of the plan.

_____

_____

Directions: Decide in advance how you will secure the answers to the above questions. Do you intend to interview human resources people in your area to determine how they have implemented an educational assistance program? Do you plan to search the Internet using terms such as educational assistance, company educational plans, or other search words/phrases?

Prepare an analysis of your plan to discuss during class. Get feedback from your classmates and instructor about the merits of your plan. Will it get you the information you need? What else do you need to do to get the answers to the questions? Formulate a final plan to present during class as directed by your instructor. Your instructor may ask you to submit a written report on this case. Use the space below to make notes concerning your plan and how you plan to implement your research. Summarize the comments and feedback of people you have asked to review your plan.

_____

_____

_____

_____

_____

_____

_____

_____

_____

_____

_____

_____

_____

_____

_____

_____

_____

_____

_____

_____

CASE STUDY 8-3: Northern Medical Center's Wage Debate

Management and employees at Northern Medical Center are battling over whether to increase employee wage rates. Management's position is that its current employee wage structure complies with governmental factors like FLSA, equal pay legislation, comparable wage rates, and market conditions. However, management has indicated to employees that business has not been good this past year and that "some jobs are in jeopardy." In general, management would like for the employees to back off on their demands.

The employees have selected a spokesman, Max Saxton, who is representing them to management. He has expressed to management that it's the employees' understanding that the company bought certain executives new cars this year and that most have gotten new office furniture as well. Further, the rumor mill has it that executives received a 10 percent to 20 percent pay raise this year, and employees want to know if that is true.

Management says that it can afford to increase wages only if greater profit is made. It is management's feeling that the productivity of employees is decreasing—perhaps intentionally —due to their discontent.

Respond to the following questions:

1. What is the general issue between management and workers in this pay conflict?

_____

_____

_____

2. If you were management, what steps would you take to resolve the stalemate?

_____

_____

_____

3. If you were Max Saxton, what would you recommend as the next step for the employees to take?

_____

_____

_____

Review the facts of the case. Do any research you need to defend your position. Write answers to the questions and be prepared to participate in a group discussion as led by your instructor or group leaders.

PROJECT 8-4: *Cafeteria Benefit Plan*

International Business Services is thinking about offering employees a cafeteria benefit plan. Mr. Francis, business operations manager, just received the premium statement for health insurance, and it has gone up 40 percent over last year's premium. He has suggested to the company president, Ms. Gibson, that perhaps the time is right to seriously consider a different benefit plan. As a result, each manager has been asked to prepare a checklist indicating the advantages and disadvantages of switching to a cafeteria benefit plan.

1. As the AOM, how would you proceed in completing this project? For example, would you seek input from your subordinates first? Why or why not? Would you call colleagues in other companies who have this benefit plan to see how it is working? Why or why not? Write a brief response to this question.

_____

_____

_____

2. Fill in the form below.

Brainstorming Checklist for Decision-Making Issue: Changing to a Cafeteria Benefit Plan	
Advantages (+)	**Disadvantages (−)**
1.	1.
2.	2.
3.	3.
4.	4.

Prepare a presentation for the class discussion and be ready to submit it to your instructor if requested.

INTERNET RESEARCH ASSIGNMENT

PROJECT 8-5: Health-Care Benefits Update

Situation: Just how much has the health-care benefit increased in cost to businesses as well as to individuals? Using an Internet search engine of your choice, key in the following key phrases or words: *Health Care Benefit* or *Managed Care Guidelines* or *HMO* or *Rise in Health Care Benefit*. Locate current data on at least three web sites.

Directions: Prepare a written report, as requested by your instructor, which reflects the most current information concerning the rise in the cost of health-care benefits. Be prepared to participate in a class discussion and share any personal experiences you or your friends have with health-care benefits and their costs.

HANDS-ON COMPUTER ASSIGNMENTS

PROJECT 8-6: Word Processing: Ranking of Benefits Offered

This activity is designed to show how three individuals view the importance of their employment benefits plan.

Complete the following tasks:

1. Retrieve PRJ08-6 from the Data CD; this file contains the table below.

2. Interview three persons about benefits they receive through their places of employment. Use Table 8-2 on page 191 in your textbook as a guide on the types of benefit (compensation) plans that might be available.

3. Ask each person to rank the top three benefits that they feel they need to receive from an employer and to describe why they ranked each as they did.

4. Print the information.

TABLE 8-1

Person's Name	Benefit #1	Benefit #2	Benefit #3
1.			
2.			
3.			

Prepare your data for submission to your instructor and as a handout for your classmates as you discuss your findings if so directed by your instructor.

HANDS-ON COMPUTER ASSIGNMENTS

PROJECT 8-7: Spreadsheet: Calculating Benefits

This activity is designed for you to practice calculating the benefits amount from a total compensation amount, given the benefits percentage.

Complete the following tasks:

1. Retrieve PRJ08-7 from the Data CD; this file contains the benefits and salary worksheet below.

2. Use formulas to calculate the amount of fringe benefits and salary, given the employee's total compensation and cost of benefits package of 37 percent.

3. Print a copy of the spreadsheet.

Employee	Total Compensation	Benefits	Salary
Corrigan	$ 31,000		
Parker	$ 38,000		
Matthew	$ 55,000		
Patrick	$ 75,000		
Kalas	$ 45,000		

Be prepared to participate in a group discussion to share your information. Your instructor may ask that you design a cover sheet and submit your information for a grade.

CHAPTER 9

HEALTH-RELATED AND OTHER WORKPLACE ISSUES

REVIEW ACTIVITY

PROJECT 9-1: Concept Quiz

Directions: For each section of the quiz below, follow the directions for that section.

Fill in the blanks with the correct word or phrase.

1. Favoritism shown to a relative in the workplace is known as _____.

2. The act passed to ensure employers with government contracts maintain a drug-free environment is called the _____ _____ _____.

3. A compulsive worker is often called a _____.

4. Most mental health experts agree that depression is best treated by a combination of _____ and _____.

5. Companies can avoid the adverse effects of several health-related and other workplace issues by _____ _____ and sending the message that management is there to help.

Circle the letter of the correct response for the following statements.

6. "Substances" in workplace policies usually means:

    A. Illegal drugs/controlled substances.
    B. Legal drugs if illegally possessed or misused.
    C. Intoxicating beverages.
    D. Mind-altering chemicals, etc.
    E. All of the above.

7. Depression is defined as:

    A. A common, debilitating condition.
    B. A state of being sad or a disorder marked by sadness, inactivity.
    C. A state of being happy and energetic.
    D. A only.
    E. A and B only.

Circle T or F for each statement that follows.

		Answers
8. Fortunately, substance abuse problems are not costly to industry or society in lost work time, health and medical expenses, or lost wages.		T F
9. An administrative manager can threaten a suspected substance abuser and argue with that employee if he or she is resistant.		T F

10. One of the factors that may be contributing to the increase in cases of depression is the rise in divorce rates. T F

11. Workaholics are generally over-stressed or worried when compared to non-workaholics. T F

12. Some states have fixed rules on smoking, as in smoking is allowed in designated areas only or not at all. T F

13. Some companies use holiday parties as family occasions that take place around lunchtime. T F

14. Increasingly, companies allow alcoholic beverages to be served at company parties. T F

15. A relative is defined as a spouse only. T F

16. Discrimination based on marital status is unlawful in most states. T F

17. Romantic relationships in the workplace can have good or bad consequences. T F

PRACTICAL EXPERIENCE ASSIGNMENTS

PROJECT 9-2: *How Would You Handle These Situations?*

Directions: Either in small groups or individually, discuss how you would solve each of the personnel problems described. Then prepare a written policy statement to cover each problem. Be prepared to justify your policy statements and to defend your answer by referring to any employment laws that pertain to these cases.

At this month's chapter meeting of the Metro Management Society, you are seated with a group of administrative managers who are discussing some of the personnel problems that faced them during the past week. You learn that not one of the companies represented has a formal policy to which the managers could turn for help in solving their problems in these situations. Consider these two situations or discussions:

A. Debits and Credits Take the Vow

The head of our accounting department announced this week that she and a clerk in her department will be getting married in three months. We've never had a married couple working in one department—in fact we've never had a married couple working in any of our offices or in the plant. I don't see how we can let the couple work together in the same department, especially since he would be reporting to her each workday. We will have to let one of them go, or possibly arrange a transfer. What do you think we should do?

Policy Statement:

The company may employ members of the same family except when one family member is responsible for supervising, or evaluating the work of another member of the family. ★ In this case the employee must be transfered or dismissed.

B. AIDS in the Workplace

This morning one of our mail clerks, Jim, came in to the office and told me he has AIDS. I offered him my full support by telling him that I surely had no objections to his continuing to work. But, you know, I fear the repercussions—the discrimination, stigma, homophobia—when others in the office get wind of his dilemma; and you know they will hear about it. What steps should my company take now?

Policy Statement:

Discrimination against any individual, such as age, color, disability, gender, race, religion, sex, or sexual orientation, is prohibited.

PROJECT 9-3: Field Research: Investigating Office Practices that Could Pose Problems

In your firm or another company in your community (your instructor will provide a list to help with the selection of different companies or you may select one with which you have experience), plan an interview with the person responsible for office policies and practices. The purpose of this interview is to determine: a) To what extent each of the office practices described below has been or is creating a problem for the firm, and; b) What action, if any, has been taken or is being studied in order to control the practice.

Directions: Answer the questions following each of the two situations subsequent to your interview. Prepare a summary paper of your findings in A and B to submit to your instructor. Be prepared to discuss your findings in class. You may want to prepare a PowerPoint presentation to illustrate your results.

A. **Office Parties and Picnics.** Many firms sponsor parties, such as at various holiday times, off the company premises. Other companies plan their holiday celebrations in the offices. Alcoholic beverages may or may not be permitted. Annual company picnics are still fairly popular as a means of bringing the "company family" together for a full day's program of planned activities—food and drink, ballgames, swimming, etc.

- To what extent does this practice create a problem for the firm?

  Most employees bring alcohol to company functions.

- What action or plan do you have to control the practice?

  Alcohol will be prohibited at all company functions and will be reprimanded with necessary disciplinary action.

B. **Giving and Receiving Gifts.** On many occasions, such as at various holidays, firms are faced with the problem of giving and accepting gifts. Some firms establish a policy of not accepting gifts that are likely to obligate the employees or the company and to give only nominal or token presents not likely to embarrass the recipient. Other firms donate to charities the money that would have been spent on holiday gifts and cards for their customers, clients, and employees.

- To what extent does this practice create a problem for the firm?

  Not giving any type of holiday gifts, the employees start to feel unappreciated.

- What action or plan do you have to control the practice?

  Give generic gifts such as gift cards.

PROJECT 9-4: Job Stress: Serious Medical Issue

Since he was hired as administrative manager, Joe Corolla has been competitive, ambitious, and aggressive. He impressed top management with his devotion to work and his expectations of perfection from himself and his coworkers. Corolla thrived on deadlines, relished risks, and lost patience when he did not reach his goals quickly. Then one day the stress of his job took its toll—a severe heart attack.

Today, Corolla's boss, Angela Miranda, leans back in her chair, reflects, and asks herself: "Why did this have to happen to a young fireball like Joe? Where did the company go wrong by not having anticipated the stresses of his job? What can we do now?"

Directions: What answers can you supply to the questions raised by Miranda?

Evaluate the facts in this case and be prepared to research the effects of stress on workers' performance and health. You will note that several athletes in perfect health (apparently) have succumbed to heart attacks or other problems during or after practice. Relate these to office workers to show any similarities. Be prepared to relate your findings in a two-page summary paper and to discuss your findings in class.

Joe worked himself to hard and probably took on more than he could handle. He also may have had a pre-existing condition, and the stress added on only triggered the condition. The stress from the job may not have been the only factor. He probably had other stress outside of work. Now you can bring him back to work but give him less responsibility and less work.

INTERNET RESEARCH ASSIGNMENTS

PROJECT 9-5: Substance Abuse in the Workplace Research

Some government and industry organizations provide resources and information to help employers make their workplaces alcohol- and drug-free. A sampling of the information provided includes many of the following topics:

Steps to a Drug-Free Workplace
Web-Based Tools
Supplies for Success
Benefits of Drug-Free Workplaces
Facts and Figures
Industry-Specific Materials
Workplace Substance Abuse Articles
Workplace Substance Abuse Posters

Directions: Access the Internet to search for information provided on one or more of the topics listed. Write a two-page paper that summarizes your findings, giving specific information as to what is provided by each company or organization, any costs involved, and ordering/shipping information. Be prepared to discuss your findings with the class. Be prepared to share any resources you have found with the class as well. Use the space below to note the web sites you visit and a summary of the information you found.

HANDS-ON COMPUTER ASSIGNMENTS

PROJECT 9-6: Word Processing: Workaholic Warning Signs

This activity is designed to observe behaviors in persons who may be workaholics.

Complete the following tasks:

1. Retrieve PRJ09-6 from the Data CD; this file contains the table below.

2. Think of someone you know who you suspect is a workaholic. Describe that person's behavior using general and specific examples and observations.

_____

_____

_____

_____

3. After you have observed the person, fill in the table below; then write a summary of your observations. Your instructor may ask you to present your findings in a class discussion and/or to submit your table and summary for grading.

Warning Sign	Behavior Observed
• No Play Time	
• Trying too Hard	
• Physical Symptoms	
• One-Track Life and/or One-Track Mind	

PROJECT 9-7: Spreadsheet: Employee Absence Analysis

This activity is designed to give you experience in creating a line graph showing trends over a two-year period.

Complete the following tasks:

1. Retrieve PRJ09-7 from the Data CD; this file contains the worksheet shown below.

2. Construct a line graph showing absence trends according to reasons for absences over a two-year period. Use appropriate titles, legends, and labels to enhance its appearance and meaning.

3. Print a copy of the spreadsheet.

Health-Related Issue	Year 1	Year 2
Illness	35	40
Substance Abuse (reported)	10	13
Stress (doctor)	20	26
Personal Reasons	15	19

Be prepared to discuss your interpretation of the information you presented in the graph. What does it mean? Which years showed an increase in absences and which reasons had the highest and lowest number of absences? Write a brief analysis of the graph to use in your discussion in class.

_____

_____

_____

_____

_____

CHAPTER 10

WORK ETHICS AND BUSINESS ETIQUETTE ISSUES

REVIEW ACTIVITY

PROJECT 10-1: Matching Terminology

Directions: In the Answers column, write the letter of the item in Column 1 that is most often associated with each item in Column 2.

Column 1	Column 2	Answers
A. Pygmalion in Management Theory	1. Deeply felt moral and ethical principles	1. ____
B. Personal space	2. Behavior that tells people how to act to meet values set by standards	2. ____
C. Basic beliefs	3. Fundamental beliefs or principles	3. ____
D. Value-driven company	4. Manager's expectations of subordinates serve as self-fulfilling prophecies	4. ____
E. Mutual loyalists		
F. Ethics	5. An attire that is appropriate for men and women; Friday casual	5. ____
G. Values	6. The flow and shift of distance between people	6. ____
H. Ethical awareness	7. One that consistently produces a high quality product or service and treats employees with respect	7. ____
I. Smart casual	8. Employees are able to recognize ethical problems when they occur	8. ____
J. Black-tie optional	9. Employees who are loyal to their employer and believe loyalty is deserved	9. ____
	10. Attire for formal occasions	10. ___

PRACTICAL EXPERIENCE ASSIGNMENTS

Project 10-2: *Ethical Situations*

Respond to the following two situations regarding ethical decisions in the workplace. Prepare an analysis of each situation and give a brief dialogue of how Situation A and Situation B should be resolved. Your instructor will direct a class discussion of each situation. Be prepared to participate in each discussion.

Situation A

When Leona Marsh passes the mailing center on the way to the workstation, she often drops several unstamped pieces of personal mail in the outgoing mail slot. Marsh feels that her company owes her this "little benefit" to compensate for all her years of service. As Marsh's supervisor, what action would you take when you learn that the company's subsidizing her postage bill?

_____

_____

_____

_____

_____

_____

_____

Situation B

Penny Ash, assistant manager of accounts payable in a large accounting department, was helping Sylvia Baum, a data-entry operator, with some month-end reports. Ash uncovered a mathematical error made by Baum and called it to her attention. Being confronted with her mistake, Baum yelled at Ash: "You're embarrassing me in front of all my coworkers. How can you do this?" As Ash, how would you respond to the screaming Baum?

_____

_____

_____

_____

_____

_____

Project 10-3:   International Issue: Child Worker Abuse

International Business Services has recently been contacted by a manufacturing organization in China. The organization needs business consulting in the area of computer set-up and operations. This is the type of business opportunity the company president, Ms. Gibson, has been hoping would happen.

Unfortunately, it has come to the attention of Ms. Gibson that this company uses children ages 10 to 16 as laborers on its production lines. No one is privileged to this information other than the four top managers at International Business Services. If you were a member of the management team, supply the following advice to Ms. Gibson about whether to do business with this international organization.

Respond to the following questions:

1. In your opinion, should the fact that this organization uses children in this way affect how International Business Services makes its money? Defend your position.

    _____

    _____

    _____

    _____

2. If (and when) the employees of International Business Services learn this information, how do you think they would advise Ms. Gibson?

    _____

    _____

    _____

    _____

3. In your opinion, do U.S. businesses have a right to express their concern over international issues of abuse such as this one?

    _____

    _____

    _____

    _____

This is a very sensitive issue. Research child labor laws in the United States and reflect on recent instances of how the United States has dealt with worker abuse in other countries that do business with the United States. Be prepared to share your research with the class in a group discussion.

INTERNET RESEARCH ASSIGNMENTS

PROJECT 10-4: *Playing Hooky in the Workplace*

Standing outside Gate F at Wrigley Field in Chicago on a recent weekday afternoon, Alan, a financial consultant who did not give his last name, was trying to be incognito in a polo shirt, shorts, and sunglasses. Alan was supposed to be at work. He told his boss that he needed a day off because he was broken up over a beloved colleague's death. It was just an excuse to play hooky.

Employees calling in sick or making up excuses to get out of work is nothing new. The problem falls on workers who show up and have to take up the absent person's duties; therefore, unscheduled absences can lead to increased workloads and stress. There have been several studies related to this costly problem for employers picking up these "mental-health" days.

Directions: As an open-ended assignment, determine the extent to which unplanned absences are a problem to businesses today. Use whatever search engine you feel appropriate. Select the search words that you think will link you to the information you need. The U.S. government's Department of Labor probably has a web site that provides current statistics or links to other information as well. When you complete your research, write a summary of the facts you learned. Be prepared to discuss your findings in class as directed by your instructor. Use the space below for notes.

_____

_____

_____

_____

_____

_____

_____

_____

_____

_____

_____

_____

_____

_____

HANDS-ON COMPUTER ASSIGNMENTS

PROJECT 10-5: Word Processing: Image Skills Observation

This activity is designed to evaluate the image skills of a businessperson.

Complete the following tasks:

1. Retrieve PRJ10-5 from the Data CD; this file contains the table below.

2. Evaluate the image skills of a person you know and see on a regular basis who works in a business organization. This could be someone in your family, a friend, a coworker, or an instructor. With this person's appearance in mind, describe five characteristics he or she consistently exhibits that reflect successful and positive image practices.

3. Print the table. Discuss your findings during a classroom discussion as directed by your instructor.

Image Detail	Description of Detail Applied Well
1.	
2.	
3.	
4.	
5.	

PROJECT 10-6: Spreadsheet: International Training Library

This activity is designed to give you experience in creating a column bar chart to compare international training media found in many organizations today.

Complete the following tasks:

1. Retrieve PRJ10-6 from the Data CD; this file contains the international culture training media worksheet shown below. Interpret the worksheet information before you start working on the bar chart. Then see how best to present the information. How do these training media compare with those used in the United States?

2. Construct and print a bar chart. Use appropriate titles, legends, and labels to enhance its appearance and meaning.

3. Be prepared to discuss your findings and your analysis in a group and then present the combined analysis to the class. You may want to use PowerPoint for your presentation, if available.

	Latin America	European	Middle East	Pacific Rim
Books	20	40	35	67
Videos	7	10	23	43
Pamphlets	45	33	54	79
Slide Shows	12	67	4	31
Internet web sites	6	54	22	33

CHAPTER 11

LEADERSHIP, MOTIVATION, AND PROBLEM-SOLVING IN ORGANIZATIONS

REVIEW ACTIVITY

PROJECT 11-1: *Matching Terminology*

Directions: In the Answers column, write the letter of the item in Column 1 that is most often associated with each item in Column 2.

Column 1	Column 2	Answers
A. Leadership	1. Emphasizes long-range planning, consensus decision-making, and strong mutual worker-employer loyalty	1. ____
B. Theory Z		
C. Personal power	2. Involves followers heavily in the decision-making process by using group involvement to set objectives, establish strategies, and determine job assignments	2. ____
D. Defensive reaction		
E. Theory Y	3. The art of enlisting people to embrace a vision or a goal as their own	3. ____
F. Participative (democratic) leader	4. The process of providing as many solutions as possible	4. ____
G. Theory X	5. Assumptions that people generally dislike work, lack ambition, and work primarily because they need to have money to live	5. ____
H. Brainstorming		
I. Generation X	6. A way of thinking that cushions the blow resulting from an immediate inability to overcome an obstacle or barrier that has been placed in your path	6. ____
J. Generation Y		
	7. The informal power that is manifested by the extent to which followers are willing to follow a leader	7. ____
	8. Assumes that work is as natural as rest or play and that workers will accept responsibility when self-direction and self-control can be used to pursue valued objectives	8. ____
	9. Born after 1977	9. ____
	10. Born between 1965 and 1976	10. ____

PRACTICAL EXPERIENCE ASSIGNMENTS

PROJECT 11-2: Misunderstanding Issue: Basking in the Florida Sun

One Friday in early January, Beth Rogers and Amy Shaw, computer operators for Flex-Shoes Inc., were discussing their plans to get some sun and attend the NCAA basketball playoffs in Orlando, Florida.

Rogers said that their hotel reservations had been made and that she was now waiting for flight confirmations. Excitedly, Shaw commented: "I'm sure glad we saved those five vacation days from last year. Come March, that gives us three whole weeks in sunny Florida." As Rogers and Shaw left work that day, they noticed that their supervisor, Hal Moser, was still at his desk. "Guess we'd better clear our plans with Hal," Rogers said to Shaw. The conversation continued:

Shaw: "Hal, Beth and I have decided to take the first three weeks in March for our vacation. You'll remember that we still have five days due us from last year."

Moser: (flustered at being interrupted in his work) "I remember. Go ahead with your plans. Just give me a note to remind me of your vacation dates. See you Monday—have a good weekend!"

On Monday afternoon, after Moser read the note indicating Rogers and Shaw's vacation dates, he interrupted their work to say: "Hey, you two! You know you can't carry your vacation time over from year to year. You should have used those five days before this year began!"

Rogers: (stunned) "But, Hal, you can't do that to us. On Friday you told us to go ahead with our plans. Don't you remember? We've made our hotel reservations, and Saturday we paid for the airline tickets. If we cancel our flight plans now, we'll be stuck with a fat penalty!"

Moser: "Guess I wasn't thinking too clearly Friday. I sympathize with you; I really do. But, look here in the employee handbook. See? It says that all vacation time must be taken during the calendar year. Employees cannot accumulate vacation time from year to year."

1. Identify the real problem in this case.

   _____

   _____

   _____

2. What is your solution to the problem you have defined?

   _____

   _____

   _____

Interview a few human resources managers to learn what companies in your area do about unused vacation time. What seems to be the norm? Prepare a paper describing your responses to each question above and submit it to your instructor. Include the research you completed in your community. Be prepared to discuss your findings in class.

PROJECT 11-3: What Type of Leader Do You Want to Be?

Directions: This activity is designed to help you identify what type of leader you would like to be. Answer the questions below to ascertain the type of leader you may become. Then write a two-page analysis that describes the type of leader you may become. Be prepared to discuss your analysis in class as directed by your instructor. You may be asked by your instructor to present a speech in class (using PowerPoint slides or transparencies if available) describing your leadership style.

1. Will I make the final decision for the group?

   _____

2. Will I allow the group members to express their opinions?

   _____

3. Will I be a charismatic leader?

   _____

4. Will I vote just to break the tie?

   _____

5. Will I let others know that I agree (or disagree) with them?

   _____

6. Will I listen to the ideas of all the members?

   _____

7. Will I try to understand before I express my agreement or disagreement?

   _____

8. Will I ask questions to get more information?

   _____

9. Will I try to minimize the tension in the group?

   _____

10. Will I stand up for myself?

    _____

11. Will I encourage others to speak?

    _____

12. Will I offer help to others?

    _____

13. Will I submit solutions to the problems?

_____

14. Will I explain the ideas of others to the group?

_____

15. Will I check for group agreement?

_____

16. Will I let others know I disagree as tactfully as possible?

_____

17. Will I ask for the opinions of others?

_____

18. Will I create an atmosphere of congeniality and informality?

_____

19. Will I sometimes agree to disagree?

_____

PROJECT 11-4: The Quiet Computer Consultant

Arthur Leon, who worked for a large computer company for several years, is now employed by International Business Services as a computer consultant. Ms. Haynes, a sales manager, senses some tension among the consultants that appears to be affecting productivity and esprit de corps. It is clear that Mr. Leon is producing and is liked very much by customers, but he appears to be happy quietly doing his job with little interaction with anyone else. Ms. Haynes has heard others call him "the loner." In asking Mr. Leon how he likes his job at International, he responds to Ms. Haynes by saying, "Oh, don't worry about me. If I didn't like it here, I can assure you I'd be gone by now."

Answer the following questions:

1. As his immediate supervisor, would you be concerned with his response? If so, in what ways? Should a person read too much into statements made in a casual manner, as the one made by Mr. Leon?

2. Is this a situation where Ms. Haynes should pursue some counseling efforts with Mr. Leon? If so, how should she proceed?

3. Do you think the consultants are being fair in their judgment of Mr. Leon? Are the consultants overreacting and not accepting Mr. Leon for the person he is?

Evaluate the facts in this case and be prepared to relate your findings in a two-page summary paper and to discuss your findings during a class discussion as directed by your instructor.

INTERNET RESEARCH ASSIGNMENT

PROJECT 11-5: Decision-Making About Employment Choices

Situation: Locate the home pages of a national company, state agency, and local company of your choice on the Internet.

Directions: Using file PRJ11-5 on your Data CD, enter the names of the companies in the first column and in one or two sentences, describe in the second column why you would want to work for this company. Based on your research, which company would you work for and how did you decide?

In other words, what is it on the home page of these organizations that would attract you toward them? It may be just a feeling you have *off the top of your head* or it may be a reason founded on a preference or value that you hold.

With those ideas in mind, go through a decision-making process and describe how you made your decision. Write a summary of the process that you followed. Your instructor may ask you to present your paper along with the information in the table in a class discussion and/or to submit your table and paper for grading.

Potential Employer	Why Work for This Company
National Company	
State Agency	
Local Company	

HANDS-ON COMPUTER ASSIGNMENTS

PROJECT 11-6: Word Processing: Problem-Solving Process

This activity is designed to review the steps in the problem-solving process. After you have completed the following tasks, be prepared to discuss why the problem-solving process works so well in our personal and professional lives. Write a brief response to this idea and be prepared to discuss your interpretation in class.

Complete the following tasks:

1. Retrieve PRJ11-6 from the Data CD. This file contains the text that is shown below.

2. Rearrange the seven steps in the problem-solving process in their logical order and number them 1, 2, 3, and so on.

3. Edit the document in the following ways:

    A. Format the topics to title case.

    B. Bold the first word of each step.

    C. Draw a box around the steps only.

4. Print a copy of the results and be prepared to discuss it in class. Your instructor may ask that you make a presentation or submit your materials for grading.

> Implementing the solution
>
> Collecting information and analyzing the problem
>
> Defining the problem
>
> Selecting the solution
>
> Monitoring progress
>
> Suggesting possible solutions
>
> Analyzing and comparing possible solutions

PROJECT 11-7: Spreadsheet: "What If" Decisions

This activity is designed to practice "what if" decision-making, using spreadsheets and a sales commission example. In addition to completing the following tasks, respond during a class discussion, upon the direction of your instructor, as to why you think spreadsheets are used by managers in the business world to create several scenarios for making decisions.

Complete the following tasks:

1. Retrieve PRJ11-7 from the Data CD; this file contains the worksheet shown below. Enter formulas to calculate net sales, commission paid on gross sales, and net income.

2. Prepare two more worksheets using these "what if" conditions:

   • Commission was increased to 15 percent of gross sales.

   • Commission was increased to 8 percent of gross sales, and gross sales decreased to $42,500.

3. Print a copy of the three worksheets. Your instructor may direct a class discussion to review net sales and commission as well as how net income is calculated. Be prepared to present your interpretations of these terms in the discussion. You may find it necessary to review these concepts in an accounting textbook. The library likely has several copies of textbooks on accounting principles. If not, ask your instructor to direct you to one.

Gross Sales	$ 45,000.00
Less Expenses	$ 21,000.00
Net Sales	
Less Commission at 5%	
Net Income	

CHAPTER 12

COMMUNICATING IN THE WORKPLACE

REVIEW ACTIVITY

PROJECT 12-1: Matching Terminology

Directions: In the Answers column, write the letter of the item in Column 1 that is most often associated with each item in Column 2.

Column 1	Column 2	Answers
A. Communication	1. A sophisticated, computerized telephone answering system that digitizes incoming spoken messages	1. ____
B. Downward Communication	2. The leader's job is to keep the meeting moving and redirect the focus of comments, but allows the group members to interact freely	2. ____
C. Grapevine	3. Communication that follows the organization's formal chain of command from top to bottom	3. ____
D. Electronic mail (e-mail)	4. Can be verbal or nonverbal responses that the receiver gives by further communicating with the original sender or another person	4. ____
E. Feedback	5. A method of conducting telephone conference calls among three or more people in different locations	5. ____
F. Group-centered approach	6. Involves transmission of information by word of mouth without regard for organizational levels	6. ____
G. Filtering	7. The exchange of messages	7. ____
H. Leader-controlled approach	8. The leader is clearly in charge at this type of meeting	8. ____
I. Voice messaging	9. The tendency for a message to be watered down or halted completely at some point during transmission	9. ____
J. Teleconferencing	10. A system that enables a user to transmit letters, memos, and other messages directly from one computer to another, where the messages are stored for later retrieval	10. ____

PRACTICAL EXPERIENCE ASSIGNMENTS

PROJECT 12-2: *Communicating Without Words*

The oldest form of human communication—nonverbal—consists of any information not spoken or written that you perceive with your senses. Some examples of nonverbal communication are gestures, facial expressions, body positions, mannerisms, tone of voice, use of physical space, and touching. In this project, you will look for such nonverbal cues in a presentation arranged by your instructor to see how the cues affect the content of the message.

Directions: Although nonverbal communication cues may last only a second or two, list all the cues that you perceive during the classroom presentation. Following the presentation, evaluate each of the cues noted by the group to learn which ones contributed positively to the communication process and which ones negatively affected the content of the message. You may be asked to discuss with the group how you noticed the cues and what impression they had on you. Your instructor will lead the discussion and may ask that you prepare a paper illustrating these cues and submit it for a grade. Use the space below to make notes during the presentation.

PROJECT 12-3: Understanding New Procedures

Willie Tadano, a new employee at International Business Services, works with other employees in the general office area. When a new procedure write-up comes to the department, it is sent around to each worker. After reading the new procedure, each worker initials the procedure and passes it along to a coworker to read.

You have noticed that Willie puts his initials on the reading materials without actually reading them. According to the other office workers, he then asks them to explain the procedure to him. Willie is such a nice person that coworkers have always wanted to help him and to make the meaning clear so he'll know how things are done.

1. What may contribute to Willie's preference not to read new information? Is there anything you would suggest to him? Is it possible that he can't read?

2. If you were the AOM, what would you do to correct this situation? If you learn that Willie can't read, what should you do? If you learn that he is just lazy, will you take another approach or would you react the same way as you would if he could not read, or if he doesn't read English very well?

This is a difficult situation for both Willie and his coworkers. Begin your work by researching English as a Second Language to learn about the difficulty of helping non-English speaking persons to understand not only the words but the meanings of those words in the context of a job setting.

In addition, research how many people in the workplace today have problems reading. What are the approaches recommended for someone who cannot read?

Hypothetically, if a person is a good worker but cannot understand instructions, what should an organization do about the situation? Brainstorm as many ideas as you can in a group setting. Be prepared to share your ideas in a class discussion as led by your instructor.

PROJECT 12-4: The International Merger with International Business Services

The owner of International Business Services has called a meeting of her management team and has explained that she is about to make a decision to "buy out" a competitor that specializes in international business consulting. If she does so, it would not only increase the staff by 15 persons, but 10 of the 15 persons from the other company are from other cultures and speak languages such as German, Spanish, Japanese, and Russian. She is asking you as part of the team to give your input about this decision she must make.

Answer the following questions:

1. In what ways can this merger be a positive move for International Business Services relative to customer service and personnel relations?

_____

_____

_____

_____

2. In what ways can this merger be a risky decision for International Business Services relative to customer service and personnel relations?

_____

_____

_____

_____

3. If you were the owner of International Business Services, what decision would you make and why?

_____

_____

_____

_____

Respond to the questions as presented above. In addition, research on the Internet additional information regarding mergers as they are conducted in the United States. Your instructor may direct a class discussion regarding this issue or ask that you prepare a paper to submit for grading. Be prepared to participate in any discussion that may ensue. Research how other companies have handled mergers that involved international businesses. One such organization was Delta Airlines when it acquired PanAmerican Airlines a number of years ago. Did they experience any problems after this merger? Research this on the Internet to add to your information when you present your report.

INTERNET RESEARCH ASSIGNMENT

PROJECT 12-5: *Research Projection Systems for Meetings*

Increasingly companies are using presentation graphics software like Microsoft PowerPoint to communicate more effectively in the workplace. A data projector device is used for this activity because it takes the image from a computer screen and projects it onto a larger screen so an audience can see the image clearly. As an administrative office manager, you may be involved in helping to make a buying decision on the best type of projection system to set up in your conference room or for managers to take on the road when making presentations away from the office.

Visit the web sites of any of the following manufacturers of focused technology and gather information by answering the questions below. The manufacturers you might research include InFocus, NEC, Proxima, Sanyo, Hewlett-Packard, or Sharp.

If possible, visit an equipment vendor in your community to view projection equipment. Ask the sales representative for any brochures or other information available. You may also want to call the manufacturers or dealers of the equipment. The web sites of the companies above may supply 800 phone numbers for customers to call.

1. How much does more brightness and resolution in the projected image cost?

   _____

   _____

2. How is brightness measured in a projector?

   _____

3. Is one manufacturer more popular than others relative to the quality of the data projector or do they seem to be about the same in ratings?

   _____

   _____

4. What is the cost range of these projector systems?

   _____

   _____

5. After researching this project, which projector would you recommend and why?

   _____

   _____

Your instructor may ask you to either prepare a class presentation (using PowerPoint, if available) or enter into a class discussion as to which model you would recommend purchasing and your reasons why.

HANDS-ON COMPUTER ASSIGNMENTS

PROJECT 12-6: *Word Processing: Downward Communication*

This activity is designed to illustrate downward communication processes in business offices and to enable you to practice editing and formatting changes.

Complete the following tasks:

1. Retrieve PRJ12-6 from the Data CD; this file contains the table below.

2. For each message in the second column, select one or more media appropriate for use in transmitting the message (i.e., group meetings, letters, e-mail, bulletin board, fax, etc.)

3. In the third column, indicate why you chose that medium.

4. Edit the document in the following ways:

    • Shade the heading row 15 percent.

    • Center the headings over each column.

    • Bullet the information you provide in the second and third columns.

5. Print a copy of the results to submit to your instructor. You may be asked to present the information in a group selected by your instructor as noted on the next page.

Message	Media	Justification
1. Company downsizing of 250 workers (plant and office) because of increased foreign competition		
2. Annual employee appraisal of an office worker		
3. Annual company bonus to be paid to all workers in their next paychecks		
4. Notice to an office worker of payroll deduction for excessive absenteeism		
5. Adoption of a new safety procedure for office workers in the reproduction center		

In a second table if directed by your instructor, interview companies in your local area to determine how they use downward communication media. Use the lines below to jot down notes as you discuss the information with each company. Then if directed by your instructor, prepare another chart to present this information or write a report if so directed in which you discuss the information you researched from the companies. If possible, prepare handouts for the class during your discussion and/or presentation.

_____

_____

_____

_____

_____

_____

_____

_____

_____

_____

_____

_____

After preparing the table (or tables) in completed form, meet informally with three other students and discuss your findings for this assignment. Your instructor may ask that you be part of a panel discussion covering these five downward communication situations.

PROJECT 12-7:   Spreadsheet: Usage Report for Communication Devices

This activity is designed to provide practice for you in creating a worksheet that reports the usage of communication devices in an organization. After following the directions indicated below, jot down some ideas to use in a class discussion that explore why you think it is important that businesses track the use of communication devices. In other words, do you think this practice is a good idea or not?

Complete the following tasks:

1. Retrieve PRJ12-7 from the Data CD; this file contains the worksheet shown below. Enter the formulas to total the number of occurrences and to determine the percentage of usage for each device.

2. Print copies of both the worksheet and the cell contents. Prepare your interpretation of the information and why you think the results indicate the usage for each device listed.

3. Do some additional research by asking a company manager in your community to respond to the usage his or her company reports for each device. If he or she has no hard and fast numbers, ask for an estimate. Then enter the information on a similar table and present the results to your instructor.

Communication Devices Usage Report		
Device	# of Uses in May	% of Uses in May
Voice Mail	767	
Fax	529	
E-Mail	987	
Totals		

CHAPTER 13

GROUP DYNAMICS, TEAMWORK, AND CONFLICT ISSUES

REVIEW ACTIVITY

PROJECT 13-1: True-False

Directions: Indicate your answer to each of the following statements by circling T or F in the Answers column.

Answers

1. Groups in general appear to have some common characteristics.   T   F

2. Groupthink is the tendency of highly cohesive groups to lose their critical evaluative abilities.   T   F

3. Hidden agendas are written lists of attitudes and feelings that individuals bring to the group.   T   F

4. For managers, virtual teams are very easy to manage.   T   F

5. When conflict occurs in organizations, it is always a very bad thing and should be avoided at all costs.   T   F

6. When identifying a problem, reframing refers to looking for evidence of a more positive view of some problem.   T   F

7. Negotiation is a psychological process requiring a give-and-take between the participants.   T   F

8. The five conflict management styles are competing, accommodating, avoiding, collaborating, and compromising.   T   F

9. The win-lose negotiating strategy assumes that one side will win by achieving its goals and the other side will lose.   T   F

10. The win-win negotiating strategy assumes that a reasonable solution can be reached that will satisfy the needs of all parties.   T   F

11. Multitasking is defined as the ability to execute more than one task over a three-hour block of time.   T   F

12. Stress in the workplace is costing American businesses staggering amounts of money.   T   F

13. Stress is not based on what happens to you, but on how you deal with what happens to you.   T   F

14. Burnout is not stress-related.   T   F

15. People who get things completed are those who prioritize their tasks and then organize them so they are easier to complete.   T   F

PRACTICAL EXPERIENCE ASSIGNMENTS

PROJECT 13-2: *Tasteless Joke Causes Conflict Between Departments*

Even in the best companies, management styles can vary from manager to manager. And those differences sometimes produce conflicts that spill over into other departments and cause problems.

That's what happened to Chuck Hodge and Heather Koger. Both ran high-performing departments, but their management styles were significantly different. Heather kept a firm hand on her department and "ran a tight ship." Chuck's style was a bit less formal, and he regularly used humor as a motivational tool.

But when Chuck cracked an inappropriate joke using one of Heather's top performers as a punch line, it threatened to create a rift between the two departments.

In Heather's department such a comment was grounds for dismissal. That was obviously not the case in Chuck's department.

Directions: What is the best way for managers to "deal with" the unique management styles that each one possesses? How do managers not get caught in the middle of conflicting standards among departments? Do you think situations such as this fictitious one happen in the workplace? Should the two managers just sit down together and discuss the problem that has been created? Jot down a few preliminary ideas below.

_____

_____

_____

_____

Following directions provided by your instructor, create some guidelines that managers can use when conflicts like this arise. Be prepared to discuss these guidelines in a class discussion. Perhaps role-playing this situation can be helpful in making you and your classmates more aware of how you talk and/or act in conflict or normal situations.

GUIDELINES

_____

_____

_____

_____

_____

_____

_____

PROJECT 13-3: Time Management: Two Scenarios

Two consultants at International Business Services were talking about not having enough time to get all their work done.

- Consultant No. 1 said, "I don't have time to plan anything."

- Consultant No. 2 said, "There is nothing I can do to manage interruptions."

Indicate your agreement or disagreement with each of these statements and explain your reasons.

_____

_____

_____

Directions: Assume you have been asked to role-play both of the statements from the consultants, but you aren't sure whether your role will be to support or refute the statements as given.

Prepare four lists of statements you would use in support of each of the four positions. After you have the four lists, indicate where you really stand on each statement. Your lists should, therefore, be organized as such:

1. Support: "I don't have time to plan anything."

    _____

    _____

2. Refute: "I don't have time to plan anything."

    _____

    _____

3. Support: "There is nothing I can do to manage interruptions."

    _____

    _____

4. Refute: "There is nothing I can do to manage interruptions."

    _____

    _____

Your instructor may lead a class discussion or allow students to be selected to role-play the situations.

PROJECT 13-4: One-Minute Strategies that Help Workers Manage Time

Here are some strategies businesspeople can use to shave off lost time and manage their efforts and energies much better. See what you think about these situations/strategies:

1. *Reply with just a fax.* Not every document requires a formal written reply. Save time by writing a response on the original and faxing it back. Take care to write in an area that will be easy to read.

2. *End with action.* Finish any planning memos with who will do what by when (participants, duties, and deadlines). Bold key dates and phone numbers.

3. *Speak up about unrealistic deadlines.* If a deadline is too short, let your boss know today, not days from now. The longer you wait, the harder it will be to roll it back.

4. *Track callbacks.* After you leave a message, jot the name of the person you called and purpose of your call on a list beside your phone. Later, when you receive that mystery greeting of "Hi, this is Tom," you won't have to wonder who Tom is and why he is calling.

Directions: Reflect on each strategy and determine if it is a strategy that you think would save workers' time, especially in the role of manager or office worker. Why do you suppose people are always looking for little ways to save time? How important is it to feel in control of how you spend your time at work?

_____

_____

_____

Prepare a brief report that evaluates each of the four strategies. Present your ideas in a short oral or written report, as requested by your instructor.

From time to time, companies present seminars in various areas around the country. One popular seminar is "Time Management." Search the Internet for seminars (or ask your instructor for any information he or she has received) and determine if this seminar is being conducted in your city or town. Another option is to telephone the local Chamber of Commerce. Chambers occasionally have business speakers who speak on various topics such as time management. Ask if any such seminar is planned for your city. Include any information you learn in your report. Use the lines below to make notes from your Internet research or when you make the telephone calls or interview the company managers in person.

_____

_____

_____

_____

_____

_____

INTERNET RESEARCH ASSIGNMENT

PROJECT 13-5: Office Organization Resources

Have you ever made statements such as these? "I've got to get organized!" Or "I'm ready for a change." Or "I'm losing so much time because I can't find anything." From time to time, probably most of us have made these statements, but what do we do about them?

The assignment in this project is for you to research several web sites to get information about how to go about organizing yourself, perhaps even how to get some help from a professional organizer. Following instructions given to you by your instructor, use the course web site below, or another one that you locate that provides information on office organization. The course site is: **http://odgers.swlearning.com**

Directions: In the web sites you visit, look for information regarding organizing solutions, products, services, and resources available to help people to become better organized. In addition, a few businesses offer organization services, from building cabinets to organizing materials in different ways to suit the owner of the business or service organization. Look in the Yellow Pages of the telephone directory to locate such a business in your city or town. Call or visit it to learn what types of services it provides. Be prepared to share any resources you have found with the class as well. Write a two-page paper that summarizes your findings, giving specific information as to what is provided and if any costs are involved. Be prepared to discuss your findings with the class.

HANDS-ON COMPUTER ASSIGNMENTS

PROJECT 13-6: Word Processing: Teamwork

This activity is designed to analyze a conflicting idea about teams.

Complete the following tasks:

1. Retrieve PRJ13-6 from the Data CD; this file contains the italicized quote below. Describe in your own words what this statement means to you. Do you agree with the statement? Compose at the computer your reaction in at least two paragraphs.

    "Teamwork in the workplace is the contradiction of a society grounded in individual achievement! And yet, team-building is in."

2. Print a copy of the results to hand in or to share in a class discussion.

Directions: Why do you think there is such an emphasis on companies to use teams as a means of getting work completed these days? Have you ever participated on a team before (sports, debate, etc.)? If so, what were the advantages to you of being on the team? Were there any disadvantages?

Either in small groups or individually, discuss your position on this topic. Then prepare to participate in a class discussion as directed by your instructor.

HANDS-ON COMPUTER ASSIGNMENTS

PROJECT 13-7: *Spreadsheet: Coping with Stress*

This activity is designed to create a simple pie chart using the Excel Chart Wizard, given the spreadsheet data shown below.

Complete the following tasks:

1. Retrieve PRJ13-7 from the Data CD; this file contains the worksheet shown below dealing with stress and the ways people cope with it in the workplace.

2. Using the data in the spreadsheet file, construct and print a pie chart. Use appropriate titles, legends, and labels to enhance its appearance and meaning.

3. Print a copy of the pie chart to share in a class discussion or to submit if so directed by your instructor.

Coping With Stress

Chat with Colleagues	33%
Take A Coffee Break	28%
Go for a Walk at Lunch	22%
Eat Some Chocolate	10%
Other	7%
Total	100%

Given the information presented in the spreadsheet and shown on the chart, discuss your interpretation of what the statistics mean. Do you think they reflect what many people do to cope with stress? Are there any additional ways you think people you know cope with stress in a constructive way? Are there ways that people cope with stress in a negative manner? Write a brief analysis of your ideas to use in your discussion in class.

CHAPTER 14

ESSENTIAL BUSINESS COMMUNICATION SKILLS

REVIEW ACTIVITY

PROJECT 14-1: Matching Terminology

Directions: In the Answers column, write the letter of the item in Column 1 that is most often associated with each item in Column 2.

Column 1	Column 2	Answers
A. Previewing	1. The official records of meetings that list the items discussed, results of votes, and responsibilities assigned to attendees.	1. ___
B. Mapping	2. A document that suggests a method for finding information or solving a problem and the methods are usually persuasive in nature.	2. ___
C. Active Listening	3. Skimming the selection while reading, looking for main points, and discovering how the material is organized.	3. ___
D. Proofreading	4. A common work/life communication tool that is available 24/7 to the user for business or personal purposes.	4. ___
E. Minutes	5. An example is the sentence: Amber is making the speech.	5. ___
F. Itinerary	6. Grouping ideas and thoughts into meaningful clusters, which helps the reader understand the hierarchy or links between the topics and concepts presented.	6. ___
G. Proposal	7. A document that is a record of travel plans.	7. ___
H. Cell phone	8. The communication process of feeding back the underlying feelings you hear as well as the content of the message.	8. ___
I. Passive Voice	9. The practice of checking for spelling, punctuation, and grammar errors in the writing process.	9. ___
J. Active Voice	10. An example is the sentence: The speech is being given by Amber.	10. ___

PRACTICAL EXPERIENCE ASSIGNMENTS

PROJECT 14-2: *Personal Phone Calls at Work*

Becky Contreras has been the receptionist at International Business Services for less than a year. Her attendance record is good, and the quality of her work and rapport with customers is also very good.

Becky comes from a family of seven brothers and sisters. It seems as if her siblings are always having problems and relying on her for advice and help. As a result, Becky is constantly receiving telephone calls at work from her family.

She was reared with a strong family commitment, so she believes all personal family problems can and should be given attention, even during work time. Besides, her customers on the phone or at her desk receive her immediate attention and also are her priority.

Respond to the following questions:

1. What do you think of Becky's attitude and beliefs in this situation?

   _____

   _____

   _____

2. Should family calls be allowed during the workday? Explain.

   _____

   _____

   _____

3. Should other personal calls be allowed during the workday? Explain.

   _____

   _____

   _____

Answer the questions that are asked. You may want to do some additional research on the way personal phone calls are handled in organizations. Interview some managers of companies in your area to learn what they do about employees receiving personal phone calls at work (on a regular basis). What seems to be the norm? Prepare a paper describing your responses to each question and submit the work to your instructor. Include the research you have completed in your business community. Be prepared to discuss your findings in class.

PROJECT 14-3: Mapping the Steps in the Writing Process

This activity is designed to help you practice using the mapping process. You will recall that mapping is a process that a reader uses to group ideas and thoughts into meaningful clusters for better comprehension. It also helps the reader understand the hierarchy or links between the topics and concepts presented in the passage being read.

Using the five steps described on pages 338-339 of the textbook, map the key ideas for each step in the writing process. Remember the mapping process is as follows: Write the main concept at the top of the page and circle it. Then, under the main concept, write, circle, and draw lines to the supporting ideas, concepts, or related vocabulary.

As a review, the five steps in the writing process are:

1. Prewriting

2. Brainstorming

3. Writing and Organizing

4. Revising for Style

5. Proofreading

Directions: Use the space below to jot down a rough sketch of mapping this assignment. Then on a separate sheet, create a more formal map of the five steps. You may want to make a plan and determine how you will present the information in class. (i.e., use PowerPoint® slides, overhead transparencies, etc.)

_____

_____

_____

_____

_____

_____

_____

_____

_____

_____

PROJECT 14-4: Removing Communication "Static" from a Business Report

Walter Black, supervisor of the administrative area of Biddie Electronics Inc., has just been handed a short report transcribed by Judy Lemcke, one of the administrative assistants. Lemcke transcribed the report exactly as it was dictated by Ed Buford, a newly hired sales correspondent. Lemcke brought the report to Black's attention since she is very concerned about the effect it will have upon Buford's boss, the sales manager. As Black reads the report, he becomes alarmed because of Buford's inability to compose his thoughts into an understandable message. The first paragraph of the one-page report is reproduced on the next page.

Directions: Rewrite the paragraph shown on page 105 so the recipient will quickly and easily understand the contents and take action. Print your revised copy using a word processing software package and hand it in to your instructor for grading. In addition, answer the following questions and be prepared to talk about them during a class discussion, which your instructor may choose to lead:

1. If you were asked to offer advice to Buford on ways to improve his overall writing ability, what are three or four suggestions you might make?

2. Do you think it is the role of the person who transcribes another's ideas in final form to critique that person's writing ability? Explain your ideas.

Using the double-spaced copy below and in your own handwriting, show corrections you would make to this paragraph. Use proofreader's markings as you edit/revise if your instructor approves. Further, in the space following the paragraph, jot down some ideas that you would use as you revise the paragraph.

In regard to your memo of the eleventh of December, which I received on my desk yesterday and which is now lying in front of me as I just got it out of my in basket, I must confess to you that I, too, am utterly distressed that the goods ordered by Jimmy Gilmore on the tenth of November under purchase order No. 6787 have not yet arrived in their warehouse nor have they received any word from us as to a late shipment or a back order. Do permit me to utilize a little time today to respond to your memo and to explain fully the innumerable difficulties that have transpired in our production facilities which have been instrumental in creating such an inordinate delay for Mr. Gilmore.

_____

_____

_____

_____

_____

_____

_____

_____

_____

_____

_____

_____

_____

INTERNET RESEARCH ASSIGNMENT

PROJECT 14-5: *Effective Listening Skills Seminar Research*

Situation: Locate the home pages of communication seminar providers or consultants of your choice on the Internet who conduct listening-skills' workshops or seminars to employees in organizations.

Directions: Using file PRJ14-5 on your Data CD, enter the names of the seminar or workshop in the first column and in one or more sentences, provide in the second column a complete description of the company or consultant offering the training, its location (near your city), the cost, content of the program, how to register, and other information you find that would be important to know. Based on your research, select a seminar to attend and explain how you made your decision.

_____

_____

In other words, what is it on the home page of these seminar providers that would attract you? It may be the way the information is presented, or it may be the completeness of the information provided.

_____

_____

With those ideas in mind, go through a decision-making process and describe how you made your decision. Write a summary of the process that you followed. Your instructor may ask you to present your paper along with the information in the table in a class discussion and/or to submit your table and paper for grading.

Name of Seminar	Description of Seminar (provider, location, cost, content, etc.)
Seminar #1	
Seminar #2	
Seminar #3	

HANDS-ON COMPUTER ASSIGNMENTS

PROJECT 14-6: Word Processing: Reading Techniques

This activity is designed to review reading techniques and to use clip art and the drawing toolbar to prepare an attractive seminar announcement. Some of the information you gathered in Project 14-5 on seminars/workshops can be utilized in this activity.

Complete the following tasks:

1. Retrieve PRJ14-6 from the Data CD. This file contains some of the text you will use and is shown below. You will need to add additional text to this announcement that you feel is necessary to promote the seminar among employees and that is fitting.

2. Prepare an attractive full-page announcement titled "Learn to Read More Effectively Workshop." Using the drawing toolbar icons in your word processing software, create an attractive announcement that would be posted on a bulletin board or circulated among employees within a company to advertise this seminar. You may use clip art, scanned photographs, word art, and any of the drawing elements and autoshapes from your word processing software to make the announcement catchy to the eye and accurately provide information to those who might want to attend. Have fun and allow yourself to be creative!

3. Print a copy of the results as directed by your instructor.

PREVIEWING

QUESTIONING

REVIEWING

MAPPING

PROJECT 14-7: Spreadsheet: Learning Retention Rates

This activity is designed for you to practice creating a bar chart that compares the average retention rates when using various learning and helping methods and techniques. In addition to completing the following tasks, explain during a class discussion, upon the direction of your instructor, why you think there are such differences among retention rates when individuals learn and retain new information.

Complete the following tasks:

1. Retrieve PRJ14-7 from the Data CD. This file contains the worksheet shown below.

2. Using the Chart Wizard and the spreadsheet information shown below that is on your Data CD, create a bar chart presenting the comparisons among various modes of learning. Use appropriate titles, legends, and grids to enhance the appearance and meaning of the content.

3. Print a copy of the bar chart and submit it to your instructor for a grade. Your instructor may direct a class discussion about the contents of this spreadsheet and explore why there is such a difference among the rates that people retain information. Evaluate how you best learn and retain information. You may also want to interview some friends and family members to gain additional information. Be prepared to present your personal ideas related to learning style and retention in a class discussion.

Average Retention Rates

Method of Learning	% of Retention
Lecture	5%
Reading	10%
Audiovisual	20%
Demonstration	30%
Discussion Group	50%
Practice by Doing	75%
Teaching Others	90%

CHAPTER 15

OFFICE DESIGN, SPACE, AND HEALTH ISSUES

REVIEW ACTIVITY

PROJECT 15-1: Matching Terminology

Directions: In the Answers column, write the letter of the item in Column 1 that is most often associated with each item in Column 2.

Column 1	Column 2	Answers
A. Office environment	1. This refers to the design of office furniture that facilitates the use of different components and variations in the way those components are arranged in the space provided.	1. ___
B. Task lighting	2. The science of designing the job to fit the worker, rather than physically forcing the worker's body to fit the job.	2. ___
C. Modular design		
D. Workflow	3. The interaction of your vision with the task that you are performing.	3. ___
E. Alternative officing	4. This illuminates the work surface.	4. ___
F. Ergonomics	5. A medical problem of the hands, specifically an inflammation of the nerve that connects the forearm to the palm of the wrist.	5. ___
G. Repetitive strain injury		
H. Visual ergonomics	6. An injury or disorder of the muscles, nerves, tendons, ligaments, and joints.	6. ___
I. Carpal tunnel syndrome	7. This is characterized by eye fatigue, blurred vision, dry eyes, and headaches.	7. ___
J. Computer vision syndrome	8. The movement of information from person to person within an organization.	8. ___
	9. Composed of several interdependent systems that include people, floor plans, furniture, equipment, lighting, air quality, and acoustics.	9. ___
	10. Flexible work arrangements and settings that support work processes, functions, or activities that can't be encompassed in one space.	10. ___

PRACTICAL EXPERIENCE ASSIGNMENTS

PROJECT 15-2: *Determining the Availability and Cost of Office Space*

Directions: In this field research project, you will investigate the marketing for office space in your hometown, or the city in which your school is located, or in another area specified by your instructor. Some of the factors to be considered in your research are offered in the list of questions below, but you may want to include others depending upon local conditions and the kind of oral or written report you are asked to prepare. Consider the following sources of information when you plan your research activities: real estate agents, banks, brokerage firms, office building developers, insurance agencies, the chamber of commerce, and your local library. Be prepared to discuss your findings in a class discussion that your instructor may choose to lead.

1. Average annual rent (or lease) per square foot of office space

_____

_____

_____

2. Availability of office space today

_____

_____

_____

3. Typical vacancy rates in office buildings

_____

_____

_____

4. Dollar volume (or square foot amount) of office building construction undertaken in the past three years

_____

_____

_____

5. Outlook for office space construction by 2008

_____

_____

_____

6. Extent of relocation of offices from center of city to less costly sites

_____

_____

7. Approximate average cost to house each office worker in a new building in the center of your community. (Allow 200 square feet per employee.)

_____

_____

8. The effect or effects that computers, telecommunications, electronic files, and telecommuting have had on office space rental and space utilization

_____

_____

_____

_____

_____

_____

_____

_____

_____

_____

PROJECT 15-3: *Evaluating the Office Environment*

In this field research project, you will evaluate the ergonomic factors in an office at your place of employment or on your campus—possibly your instructor's office. You will have an opportunity to study several elements of the office environment, appraise each one on the rating scale provided, and offer your recommendations for improvement. Following your investigation of the office environment, you may be asked to present your research findings in a written report or oral presentation (using PowerPoint, if desired).

Directions: Examine the office of your choice in relation to each of the environments described below. Access PRJ15-3 on your Data CD and print the table to use in your evaluation visit. In Column 2 of the table, evaluate the ergonomic effectiveness of the environment; in Column 3, offer suggestions for improving the environment you visited. If approved by your instructor, evaluate the environment in a new office building or other facility in your area. You may find it interesting to evaluate the lighting and other environmental features from the table below in a restaurant as well.

Environments	Rating Scale Poor ⟷ Excellent	Recommendations
Office Lighting		
• Glare	0 1 2 3 4 5	
• Proper lighting systems that may include:		
• Task/ambient lighting	0 1 2 3 4 5	
• Natural light	0 1 2 3 4 5	
• Fluorescent lighting	0 1 2 3 4 5	
• Incandescent lighting	0 1 2 3 4 5	
Color/Decor		
• Color provides aesthetic value	0 1 2 3 4 5	
• Color provides functional value	0 1 2 3 4 5	
• Color tends to create moods	0 1 2 3 4 5	
Noise		
• Hazards to the ears	0 1 2 3 4 5	
• Annoyance to workers of loud sounds	0 1 2 3 4 5	
Air Control		
• Temperature control	0 1 2 3 4 5	
• Air quality	0 1 2 3 4 5	

PROJECT 15-4: Brainstorming Ideas in the Classroom Environment

Students and instructors often express the opinion that learning and teaching would be enhanced if the classroom presented an environment wherein both students and teacher were motivated to be more productive. Like a business office, a classroom has its own psychological and physiological environmental needs. In this project, you will examine several environments of your classroom as you take part in a brainstorming session.

The problem to be solved is this: *What can be done to improve the environmental factors in our classroom?*

Directions: Your instructor will divide the class into groups of four to seven people and set a time limit of 15 to 25 minutes for the brainstorming session. During this time, each group will generate ideas for improvements in each of the following classroom environments:

1. *Office Lighting* environment (glare and lighting systems)

2. *Color Décor* environment (aesthetic value, functional value, and affect on mood)

3. *Noise environment* (sources of noise, noise control)

4. *Air Control* environment (temperature, air quality, humidity, cleanliness)

The members of each group are to present ideas off the tops of their heads, with no concern about the quality of ideas presented. The objective is to generate a great quantity of ideas by being very imaginative and possibly "hitching a ride" on the ideas presented by other classmates. Any idea is welcome as long as it may be used for discussion purposes.

As you begin, keep the following points in mind:

• There is to be no criticism or evaluation of ideas.

• No one is to be complimented on the idea presented.

• There are to be no questions or discussion regarding the ideas while brainstorming is occurring.

One person should be selected by each group to serve as recorder. This person will record all ideas presented by the group members, regardless of whether or not the ideas appear valuable. The person serving as recorder is responsible for seeing that the rules noted above are followed and that the group stays on target during the time limit set by your instructor.

The instructor will set the due date for collecting the transcription of each group's ideas. The instructor, either acting alone or aided by other faculty members or students, can evaluate the economic feasibility of the ideas presented. At a later date, a report may be made to the class of those ideas that merit being passed along to the appropriate individuals on campus for evaluation.

INTERNET RESEARCH ASSIGNMENT

PROJECT 15-5: Office Design and Layout

Situation: Locate the home pages of an architectural and/or office-oriented magazine, journal, or association of your choice on the Internet that deals with topics of office design and layout. You may want to use a search engine of your choice to locate these home pages by keying in office design, office layout, office trends, office structures, and others you may select.

Directions: Using file PRJ15-5 on your Data CD, enter the sources of the information you are reporting on in the first column and in two or three sentences, provide in the second column a description of the fact, trend, and/ or statistic you located in the source.

With those descriptions in mind, write a summary of the best ideas you located. Your instructor may ask you to present your paper along with the information in the table in a class discussion and/or to submit your table and paper for grading.

Source of Information	Description of Fact, Trend, and/or Statistic
1.	
2.	
3.	

HANDS-ON COMPUTER ASSIGNMENTS

PROJECT 15-6: Word Processing: The Failed Fire Inspection

This activity is designed for you to create an action plan that a company must use to correct three serious fire hazards that exist in the administrative offices. The local fire department just left the offices and informed you, as the administrative office manager, that an action plan for each hazard must be written and/or in place before their re-inspection visit next week.

Complete the following tasks:

1. Retrieve PRJ15-6 from the Data CD. This file contains the text in the table below. As the AOM, you have been asked to complete the written action plan before the inspector's visit for each of the three hazards that were identified.

2. In Column 3 of the table, compose at the computer a brief action plan for correcting each hazard. You may want to consult with the local fire department or discuss with classmates your ideas before creating and submitting your plan in writing. Determine if this is a typical practice for fire departments to perform inspections of this type in the city. In your opinion, is this practice of inspections a waste of the taxpayers' money? Explain your opinion.

3. Print a copy of the table showing your suggestions and action plan. Be prepared to explain your ideas in a class discussion, if appropriate. Your instructor may ask that you make a presentation or submit your materials for grading.

Office Hazards — Observed and Action Plan to Correct		
Hazard	**Description of Hazard**	**Proposed Action Plan**
#1	Too many stacks of paper on top of desks, shelves, and windowsills in offices. When asked, the office workers said there weren't enough shelves or filing cabinets in the organization.	
#2	In some offices, near the computer workstations, there are mazes of cabling, extension cords, and multiple cord adapters. Some cords appear to be showing signs of wear and are beginning to fray.	
#3	There is an inadequate number of fire extinguishers located in well-marked, accessible locations.	

PROJECT 15-7: *Spreadsheet: Accident Costs*

This activity is designed for you to create a departmental accident cost report that will show not only on-the-job hours lost but also total costs incurred associated with monetary losses. In addition to completing the following tasks, explain during a class discussion, upon the direction of your instructor, the reasons you think managers in the business world use spreadsheets and graphs to analyze cost data on workplace accidents. Your instructor may ask you to submit the materials for a grade as well as use them in a class discussion.

Complete the following tasks:

1. Retrieve PRJ15-7 from the Data CD; this file contains the worksheet shown below.

2. Use formulas to calculate totals for each column and each row.

3. Plot the total-costs column on a 3-D horizontal bar graph by department; add a chart title and vertical grids as appropriate.

4. Print the graph in color, if you have a color printer.

Accident Cost Report for January			
	Work Hours Lost	**Average Cost per Hour**	**Total Costs**
Personnel	40	$9.00	
Manufacturing	120	$10.00	
Marketing	20	$12.00	
Total			

CHAPTER 16
MANAGING WORKPLACE SAFETY

REVIEW ACTIVITY

PROJECT 16-1: True-False

Directions: Indicate your answer to each of the following statements by circling T or F in the Answers column.

Answers

1. Workplace violence is any physical assault, threatening behavior, or verbal abuse occurring in the work setting. T F

2. There are only two types of workplace violence. T F

3. Violence by strangers involves verbal threats, threatening behavior, or physical assaults by an assailant who has no legitimate business relationship to the workplace. T F

4. Violence by someone you know includes a current or former spouse, lover, relative, friend, or acquaintance and involves verbal threats, threatening behavior, or physical assaults. T F

5. A risk factor is a condition or circumstance that may increase the likelihood of violence occurring in a particular setting. T F

6. It is only a suggestion that companies should develop a crisis management program, because the majority of companies will not be in need of one. T F

7. A hazard assessment is a step-by-step, common-sense look at the workplace to find existing or potential hazards that could result in workplace violence. T F

8. Most companies do not see the need for training and instruction about preventing workplace violence because it is just common sense to the majority of workers. T F

9. A written policy provides the foundation for successful safety programs and can help avoid the expense and other consequences of workplace accidents by making sure that employees know what is expected of them. T F

10. In addition to a basic safety policy, an explicit policy regarding domestic violence in the workplace helps ensure increased workplace safety. T F

11. An employer should conduct a background check only on those job applicants who look like they might become violent. T F

12. The Fair Credit Reporting Act is designed to promote accuracy and ensure the privacy of the information used in background checks. T F

13. Should you suspect that someone could turn violent in your office, confront them as soon as possible. T F

14. The five warning signs of escalating violent behavior in a person are confusion, frustration, blame, anger, and hostility. T F

15. Companies should proactively set up policies and procedures for responding in the aftermath of a violence incident in the workplace. T F

PRACTICAL EXPERIENCE ASSIGNMENTS

PROJECT 16-2: Handling a Crisis Situation

An elderly client who was in a conference with a consultant at International Business Services suddenly developed severe chest pains. As the administrative office manager, you were the first person the consultant saw as he ran down the hall seeking help.

Directions: Your instructor will divide the class into groups of four to seven people and set a time limit of 15 to 25 minutes for the brainstorming session. During this time, each group will generate ideas for handling a crisis situation, both positively and negatively.

As a reminder about the brainstorming process, the members of each group are to present ideas off the tops of their heads, with no concern about the quality of ideas presented. The objective is to generate a huge quantity of ideas by being very imaginative and possibly "hitching a ride" on the ideas presented by other classmates. Any idea is welcome as long as it may be used for discussion purposes.

One person should be selected by each group to serve as recorder. The person serving as recorder is responsible for seeing that the group follows proper brainstorming procedures and stays on target during the time limit. As a result of your brainstorming session, fill in the following check sheet, indicating what actions you would take and those you would not take in handling this crisis. Prepare to explain your ideas in a class discussion or oral presentation as specified by your instructor.

Brainstorming Check Sheet Handling An Office Crisis	
Actions To Take	*Actions Not To Take*

PROJECT 16-3: *Emergency Preparedness Survey*

Emergencies, disasters, accidents, injuries, and crime can occur without warning at any time. Being physically and psychologically prepared to handle unexpected emergencies is an individual, as well as an organizational, responsibility. In this field research project, you will evaluate the emergency preparedness practices used by three companies, schools, or government offices in your town.

Directions: Contact three organizations of your choice and ask questions to find out the steps they have taken to prepare their employees for workplace emergencies. Using the table on the following page, jot down the responses you received to the questions you asked. Following your investigation, use the completed table of information to prepare your research findings in a written two-page report. You may be asked by your instructor to present your research findings in an oral presentation (using PowerPoint, handouts) as well. Use the space below to record the names of the organizations you plan to call, the telephone numbers, contact persons, best time to call for information (if stated), and the addresses (if needed).

_____

_____

_____

_____

_____

_____

_____

_____

_____

_____

_____

Emergency Preparedness Survey			
Question	**Organization #1 Responses**	**Organization #2 Responses**	**Organization #3 Responses**
Does your organization have an emergency procedures handbook available in the work area that is readily accessible for all employees?	Yes or No Explain:	Yes or No Explain	Yes or No Explain
Do you have exits clearly marked in the case of an emergency so employees and customers know where the nearest exit is and the best route to follow when leaving the premises?	Yes or No Explain:	Yes or No Explain:	Yes or No Explain:
Do employees know where the fire extinguishers are located throughout the building?	Yes or No Explain:	Yes or No Explain:	Yes or No Explain:
Do employees know whom to call in an emergency (such as flooding, civil disturbance, medical emergency, hazardous materials spill, fire, bomb threat)?	Yes or No Explain:	Yes or No Explain:	Yes or No Explain:

PROJECT 16-4: The Unwanted Visitor

One day an odd fellow walked into the offices of International Business Services. Becky Contreras, the receptionist, greeted this visitor initially with kindness and asked if she could help him, but she suddenly got frightened. The person had a menacing attitude, was unkempt, and mumbled badly when he spoke. Over the past few days, she had noticed him walking up and down the street, with no apparent intention of coming into the offices.

When Becky politely, but firmly, asked the person to wait so she could contact an executive, he opened the front door, looked back at her in an irritated way, and intentionally slammed the front door shut very hard as he left. Becky immediately ran to the administrative manager's office, very shaken and almost in tears. She asked what she should have done. She is afraid he will return. Becky asks if she should lock the front door to the office and call the police.

Directions: Evaluate the facts in this case and be prepared to relate your findings in a two-page summary paper and to explain your findings during a class discussion directed by your instructor. If you were the AOM, how would you answer Becky's questions? As the receptionist, did Becky handle the situation wisely? Explain the reasons for your choice. As a matter of effective policy and procedure, what actions should International Business Services take now and in the future to deal with emergency situations of this type? You may want to research web sites concerning threatening workplace situations to augment your findings. Use the space below for notes, procedures, web sites you have visited, and other information you think you will need or have found. You may want to interview one or two human resources managers or office managers to get their input for your paper if directed to do so by your instructor.

_____

_____

_____

_____

_____

_____

_____

_____

_____

_____

_____

INTERNET RESEARCH ASSIGNMENT

PROJECT 16-5: Guns in the Workplace

Situation: Assume your company has asked you to serve on a task force that is charged with the assignment of developing a new policy on the safety issue of prohibiting employees from bringing guns to work as well as preventing employees from keeping guns in their locked motor vehicle. You have volunteered to research on the Internet the current thinking of organizations across the country on this issue. A member of your task force team indicated to you that he thought some states have or are contemplating passing bills that would permit individuals who have undergone a background check and training to have a license to carry a concealed gun. Therefore, you might want to search legislative bills dealing with guns and workplace violence issues. In addition, an interview with local law enforcement officials may give you input as to their direction when dealing with guns in the workplace or on company property.

Directions: Using file PRJ16-5 on your Data CD, enter the title of the article and publication name or web site address where you located your information. Then in the second column, provide a synopsis of the important information that you will be sharing with your task force. Based on your research, which information in the articles you reviewed most represents your personal point of view and that of your task force?

_____

_____

_____

_____

Your instructor may ask you to present your findings in a report format along with the information in the table in a class discussion and/or to submit your table and report for grading.

Article and Publication or web site Visited	Synopsis of Article Relative to Prohibiting Guns at Work
1.	
2.	
3.	

HANDS-ON COMPUTER ASSIGNMENTS

PROJECT 16-6: Word Processing: Policy Writing

This activity is designed to review the purpose and key themes of the two policies presented in Chapter 16; namely, the Workplace Safety Policy shown in Figure 16.1 and the Domestic Violence in the Workplace Policy outlined in Figure 16.2. After you have completed the following tasks, be prepared to discuss why policy preparation is a critical activity to perform in organizations. Write a brief response to this concept and be prepared to discuss your interpretation in class.

Complete the following tasks:

1. Retrieve PRJ16-6 from the Data CD. This table file contains the text that is shown below.

2. In your own words, write a simple purpose of the two policies in Column 2. Then in Column 3, provide at least four key themes in each policy that are significant for employees to know.

3. Print a copy of the results and be prepared to discuss your synopsis in class. Your instructor may ask that you make a presentation or submit your materials for grading.

Safety Policies in Organizations		
Policy	**Purpose**	**Key Themes (4)**
Workplace Safety Policy		1.
Domestic Violence in the Workplace Policy		1.

PROJECT 16-7: Spreadsheet: Security Report

This activity is designed for you to practice preparing a security report and a comparison line chart to include in the annual security report to the governing board at a local community college. In addition to completing the following tasks, respond during a class discussion upon the direction of your instructor why you think charts are favorable in presenting statistical data to a decision-making group of this type.

Complete the following tasks:

1. Retrieve PRJ16-7 from the Data CD; this file contains the worksheet shown below.

2. Calculate the total number for each type of offense in the last column of the spreadsheet. Then, using the Chart Wizard and the information shown below, prepare a line chart comparing the campus crime offenses over the three-year period. Use appropriate titles, legends, and grids to enhance the appearance and meaning of the content. Print the chart and be prepared to share the information with the class and/or to submit it to your instructor for grading.

Campus Crime Statistics

Offense	**Public Property**			
	2004	2003	2002	Total
Aggravated Assault	2	1	4	
Arson	0	0	2	
Burglary	15	10	12	
Drug-Related Violations	20	15	29	
Liquor Law Violations	29	22	18	
Motor Vehicle Theft	1	0	2	
Robbery	1	3	2	
Sex Offenses	10	4	6	
Weapons Possession	5	6	3	

CHAPTER 17

OTHER WORKPLACE PRODUCTIVITY SYSTEMS

REVIEW ACTIVITY

PROJECT 17-1: Matching Terminology

Directions: In the Answers column, write the letter of the item in Column 1 that is most often associated with each item in Column 2.

Column 1	Column 2	Answers
A. Records management	1. A computerized telephone system that allows callers to leave messages.	1. ___
B. Document feeder	2. Provides document security by destroying sensitive material to ensure that it stays confidential.	2. ___
C. Voice mail	3. A large, flat table with a small lip around three or four sides used for visual inspection of mail before individual handling.	3. ___
D. Unified messaging systems	4. Allows you to copy multi-page documents without having to lift and lower the platen cover for every sheet you copy.	4. ___
E. Mail dump table	5. Irreplaceable documents, such as property deeds, copyrights, leases, contracts, and other legal documents that are typically kept permanently.	5. ___
F. Accounting cycle	6. Documents, such as internal memos and correspondence, that can be destroyed when their purpose is accomplished.	6. ___
G. Shredder	7. Involves recording, classifying, and summarizing financial information for owners, managers, and other interested parties.	7. ___
H. Vital records	8. Consists of index-card-sized film that can be read on a variety of readers or printed out in the form of paper enlargement.	8. ___
I. Nonessential records	9. Deals with the control, retention, and security of records and files whether in paper or electronic form.	9. ___
J. Microfiche	10. Gives users a convenient way to retrieve their e-mail, voice mail, and fax messages.	10. ___

PRACTICAL EXPERIENCE ASSIGNMENTS

PROJECT 17-2: *Consolidating Mailing Activities*

As AOM at International Business Services, you have received several advertisements from a new business in town called Ajax Mailing Services. They want you to consider outsourcing and consolidating all your mailing/shipping activities at International Business Services by giving your entire mailing/shipping business to them. They believe that your mailing costs will be reduced by at least 10 percent if you do consolidate. Ajax Mailing Services will provide overnight service, pickup twice a day, and bill you on a monthly basis.

You are now using the U.S. Postal Service, UPS, and, at times, Federal Express for your related mailing/shipping services.

Complete the following tasks:

1. Fill in the following check sheet, showing the advantages and disadvantages of consolidating all mailing/shipping activities with Ajax Mailing Services. You may want to do some additional research on the services provided by the U.S. Postal Service, UPS, and Federal Express.

2. Interview a few organizations in your area to learn what companies in your area do about outsourcing mailing/shipping services. What seems to be the norm?

3. Prepare a paper describing your responses to both the advantages of consolidating mailing/shipping services and the disadvantages you've identified and submit the paper to your instructor. Include the research you have completed in your community. Be prepared to discuss your findings in class.

Brainstorming Check Sheet for Decision-Making Issue: Consolidating Mailing/Shipping Activities with Ajax Mailing Services	
Advantages (+)	**Disadvantages (–)**

PROJECT 17-3: Office Copying Processes

In completing this field research project, you will investigate the copying processes in your own company, on your campus, or in a business within your community. You will evaluate the copying processes that are provided and determine under what conditions one process is selected in preference to another. The visit should also enable you to see some of the equipment in action (decentralized copiers, centralized copying areas, multi-function devices, etc.) and to talk with equipment operators to learn about the kinds of problems found on the job. Your instructor may assign a team of students to undertake this project and have them report back to the class orally or in a written report. If possible, evaluate more than one company's copying process.

Directions: Using the form on the next page, evaluate each of the copying processes according to the following factors:

1. *Appearance of Copy.* Is the copying process limited to reproduction of one color or may several colors be copied? Can pictures and line drawings be satisfactorily copied? Can pages from a bound volume be copied legibly?

2. *Length of Run.* What is the most economical range in number of copies for each process? Has a cutoff point been set with reference to economy of run for each process?

3. *Copy Size and Paper Size.* What is the maximum size of the original that can be copied? What is the maximum size of paper stock that can be used for producing copies? Can copies be reduced or enlarged in size? Can a copy be printed on both sides of the sheet in one operation (duplexing)?

4. *Copy Cost.* Can plain paper be used or must special copy paper be purchased? What special supplies are required for equipment operation?

5. *Speed of Output.* How many copies can be produced per minute? Are documents automatically fed into the copier or must they be manually inserted? Are copies automatically collated? Are they automatically stapled? What is the usual turnaround time for those requesting copies?

6. *Ease of Operation.* How much training is required before a worker can operate the copier satisfactorily? Is the equipment subject to frequent jamming? Is the paper stock easily loaded into the equipment? Is the equipment subject to excessive downtime? Are any equipment operations messy and thus cause smudges or stains on the operator's hands or clothing? Is someone designated as the key operator to call should there be a copier problem before calling a service technician?

7. *Control over Operations.* Is the copying equipment kept in one central location or do you find copiers scattered throughout the office? Is the equipment available for personal use on company time? Does the company have a charge-back system whereby reproduction costs are charged back to the department or division requesting copies? What evidence of copier misuse (personal use, reproduction of copyrighted materials without permission, excessive waste, etc.) do you find? Are operators required to keep a log of all work produced or do the workers? What security is provided for the reproduction of confidential documents? Are copiers kept locked with access only by authorized operators who must have a key, access card, or special number code?

Factors To Investigate	Office Copying Processes (Specify the Kinds of Copiers)
1. Appearance of Copy	
2. Length of Run	
3. Copy Size and Paper Size	
4. Copy Cost	
5. Speed of Output	
6. Ease of Operation	
7. Control over Operations	

PROJECT 17-4: Getting Acquainted with the Telephone Directory

You have probably "let your fingers do the walking" through the Yellow Pages, but how often have you consulted the Customer Guide pages of your local telephone directory? Much valuable information and cost-reducing suggestions may be obtained by studying the Customer Guide pages, which are often placed in the first section of the directory.

Directions: Consult your local telephone directory to find answers to the following questions. If there isn't any information related to a particular question, provide some additional information you learned as a result of this project. Your instructor may ask that you be prepared to discuss your findings in a class discussion.

1. Under what conditions is it legal to wiretap or otherwise intercept a telephone call?

   _____

   _____

2. Explain the operation of three-way calling service.

   _____

   _____

3. What steps should you take to handle obscene, threatening, or harassing calls?

   _____

   _____

4. What federal and state taxes and surcharges apply to your telephone calls and equipment use?

   _____

   _____

5. What services are provided for customers with disabilities?

   _____

   _____

6. What does the "pay per call" service mean (i.e., use of "976" and "900" numbers)?

   _____

   _____

INTERNET RESEARCH ASSIGNMENT

PROJECT 17-5: Decision-Making About A Shredder Purchase

Situation: Locate the home pages of companies on the Internet that sell a variety of shredders. Compare the features of three shredders of your choice and determine which one you would recommend purchasing for a corporate law firm office of approximately 50 attorneys, paralegals, and administrative staff members.

Directions: Using file PRJ17-5 on your Data CD, enter the names of the web site companies in Columns 2, 3, and 4. For each shredder, evaluate its appropriateness for the above-described law firm based on the six features listed. Based on your research, which shredder would you recommend the company buy because it best fits the firm's needs?

With those ideas in mind, go through a decision-making process and describe how you made your decision. Write a summary of the process that you followed. Your instructor may ask you to present your paper along with the information in the table in a class discussion and/or to submit your table and paper for grading.

Features	Shredder #1 Name Feature Evaluation	Shredder #2 Name Feature Evaluation	Shredder #3 Name Feature Evaluation
1. Throat Size			
2. Sheet Capacity			
3. Speed			
4. Staple/Paper clip Disposition			
5. Shred Size and Cut Type			
6. Cost			

HANDS-ON COMPUTER ASSIGNMENTS

PROJECT 17-6: *Word Processing: Records Management Systems*

This activity is designed to help you determine the sophistication of records management among a few selected organizations in your community. After you have completed the following tasks, be prepared to discuss which company has the most effective records management system and why, in your opinion, it does.

Complete the following tasks:

1. Retrieve PRJ17-6 from the Data CD; this file contains the table below.

2. Survey two businesses in your community to determine how they have set up their records management systems. Using the list of questions in the table, interview each business over the phone or in person.

3. From your interview responses, key the results of your survey in the following table, and print. Your instructor may ask that you make a presentation or submit your materials for grading.

Questions	Business #1	Business #2
Is there an individual in your company who is responsible for maintaining your records management system?		
Do you have procedures established to remove old files and store or destroy them?		
Does your company use any type of electronic storage, e.g., microfiche, microfilm, company output microfilm, or optical storage on CDs?		
What percentage of your filing activities is paper filing in file cabinets?		

PROJECT 17-7: Spreadsheet: Storage System Comparisons

This activity is designed to enable you to practice calculating overall averages in order to spot trends in the use of an organization's electronic and paper storage system. In addition to completing the following tasks, respond during an instructor-led class discussion on why you think some departments in organizations are more apt to store files electronically rather than on paper.

Complete the following tasks:

1. Retrieve PRJ17-7 from the Data CD; this file contains the worksheet shown below.

2. Use formulas to calculate the overall average percentage of each type of storage. The row line indicating average percentages should be boxed in using 14-point bold-italic type style.

3. Create a 3-D vertical bar graph showing the comparison of paper and electronic storage. Use appropriate titles, legends, and grids in your final printout.

4. Print a copy of the worksheet and bar graph. Be prepared to discuss or demonstrate your findings graphically as directed by your instructor.

Department	% Paper Storage	% Electronic Storage
Business Office	37%	63%
Human Resources	41%	59%
Customer Service	59%	41%
Average		

CHAPTER 18

COMPUTER NETWORK SYSTEM AND SECURITY ISSUES

REVIEW ACTIVITY

PROJECT 18-1: *Matching Terminology*

Directions: In the Answers column, write the letter of the item in Column 1 that is most often associated with each item in Column 2.

Column 1	Column 2	Answers
A. Telecommunications	1. Made up of several devices (computers, terminals, or other hardware devices) connected by an electronic communication system.	1. ___
B. Fiber optics		
C. Videoconferencing	2. A computer device and part of the LAN that allows for sharing of peripheral devices such as printers and hard-disk storage units.	2. ___
D. Computer network		
E. Local area network	3. The transfer of data from one place to another over communication lines or channels.	3. ___
F. File server		
G. Intranet	4. The user identification given to a worker by the network system administrator.	4. ___
H. User name	5. Also called Wi-Fi, it connects a desktop transmitter to a DSL or cable modem.	5. ___
I. Wireless network		
J. Firewall	6. A computer and communications network that covers a limited geographic area.	6. ___
	7. A type of security system consisting of hardware and/or software that prevents unauthorized access to data, information, and storage media on a network.	7. ___
	8. Roughly the diameter of human hair, it can transmit as many as 1 billion bits of information per second in the form of digitized pulses of light.	8. ___
	9. A meeting between two or more geographically separated people who use a network or the Internet to transmit audio and video data.	9. ___
	10. A company's internal network that makes company information accessible to employees and facilitates working in groups.	10. ___

PRACTICAL EXPERIENCE ASSIGNMENTS

PROJECT 18-2: The E-Mail Crunch

The marketing department has called a special departmental meeting as a result of complaints from the three sales secretaries. The secretaries' concern is that the e-mail system is just not working. They report that only three out of the 12 sales representatives at International Business Services check their e-mail on a regular basis. The procedure is for secretaries to interface by phone or in person with customers if the sales representative is not available. The secretary is to send an e-mail message to the sales representative regarding the customer's concern or concerns. In the past week, more than 20 irate customers have called and complained that their sales representative never got back to them.

Respond to the following questions:

1. Identify the real problem in this case.

_____

_____

_____

2. What is your solution to the problem you have defined?

_____

_____

_____

3. What are some areas of concern in using e-mail? Do you feel this problem at International Business Services is realistic in today's business world? Explain.

_____

_____

_____

4. What steps can an organization take to ensure the proper usage of e-mail systems by office and sales staff?

_____

_____

_____

PROJECT 18-3: The Internet's Effect on Business

This activity is designed to help you have a better understanding of the Internet and its effect on the way businesses operate. The Internet has had a tremendous influence on businesses. For some businesses, that influence has not been positive. For example, a growing number of people make their own travel plans online, and travel agents are seeing fewer customers as a result.

Directions: Work with a group of your classmates as assigned by your instructor and complete the following team exercise. Using the form provided below, have each member of your team interview a businessperson who is or has been affected negatively by the Internet or Internet access. You may access PRJ18-3 on the Data CD to print the form if you wish. Record the responses because you will use them to recap and prepare a written team paper summarizing your findings. You may be asked by your instructor to create a group PowerPoint presentation and share your findings with the class.

Questions	Responses
1. What positive effect(s) has the Internet had on your business?	
2. What negative effect(s) has the Internet had on your business?	
3. How can your business compete effectively with competitors on the Internet?	
4. Does the fact that nobody owns the Internet concern you and the future of your business?	

PROJECT 18-4: How Local Area Networks Work

Many schools and offices have a local area network (LAN) connecting their computers. This is one of the best setups that allows for the sharing of files, equipment, and other resources on a computer system to maximize efficiency and effective work flow among employees.

Directions: As a field research activity, work with a group of your classmates as assigned by your instructor and complete the following team exercise. Using the form provided below, have each member of your team locate a school or office that uses a network and talk to someone about how their network functions. You may access PRJ18-4 on the Data CD to print a copy of the form if you wish. Record the responses because you will use them to recap and prepare a written team paper summarizing your findings. You may be asked by your instructor to create a group PowerPoint presentation and share your findings with the class.

Questions	Responses
1. What communications technology do you use?	
2. When did you set up your local area network? What improvements have you made since that initial installation of the LAN?	
3. What are the advantages of having a network?	
5. What are the disadvantages of having a network?	
6. Is the network connected to another network? If so, how?	
7. How do you see your organization improving the current LAN system?	

INTERNET RESEARCH ASSIGNMENT

PROJECT 18-5: Protecting Your Computer From Viruses

Some viruses are harmless pranks that simply freeze a computer temporarily or display sounds or messages. Other viruses destroy or corrupt data stored on the hard disk of the infected computer. If you notice any unusual changes in your computer's performance, it may be infected with a virus. You can protect your computer at home or at work from viruses as follows: 1) by installing an anti-virus program and then periodically updating the program by connecting to the manufacturer's web site; and 2) by following simple measures that safeguard and protect your computer.

Respond to the following questions:

1. Do I back up my important files regularly? If so, how? Explain.

   _____

   _____

2. Do I have an anti-virus software program installed on my computer to regularly scan for viruses? Do I keep it updated on a regular basis?

   _____

3. Do I limit myself to open only those e-mail attachments that I am expecting from a trusted source?

   _____

4. Do I always make sure that I never start a computer with a floppy disk in drive A (as that is one of the major ways viruses are spread)?

   _____

Directions: An anti-virus program scans memory, disks, and incoming e-mail messages and attachments for viruses and attempts to remove any viruses it finds. Visit two of the more popular anti-virus web sites on the Internet that make and sell the following two products: McAfee VirusScan and Norton AntiVirus. In addition, use a search engine of your choice to find a third anti-virus program.

Using the table on the next page, respond to each question regarding the three anti-virus programs. Based on your research findings, which anti-virus program would you recommend a company buy? On what did you base your decision primarily?

Your instructor may ask you to present your paper along with the information in the table in a class discussion and/or to submit your table and paper for grading.

Questions	McAfee VirusScan Software	Norton AntiVirus Software	Other Anti-Virus Software
1. What features does the product have that organizations would desire?			
2. What is the process you follow to keep the anti-virus program updated on a regular basis?			
3. What is the initial cost of acquiring this software as well as the continuous charges over time of keeping the software updated with new anti-virus program updates?			

HANDS-ON COMPUTER ASSIGNMENTS

PROJECT 18-6: Word Processing: Networked Computer Systems

This activity is designed so that you will survey business usage of networked computer systems in your community and format the information in a multi-column table format. Contact at least two businesses in your community to determine how each uses computer networks and communication systems and if they have experienced any computer risks during the past few years. Using the following list of questions as a guide, you may interview each business over the phone or in person. After you have completed the following tasks, be prepared to explain your findings in a class discussion, as outlined by your instructor.

Complete the following tasks:

1. Retrieve PRJ18-6 from the Data CD; this file contains the table shown below.

2. From your interview responses to the following four questions, key the results of your survey in the following table and print.

Questions	Business #1	Business #2
Are your computers networked? If so, are they peer-to-peer, server-based, etc.?		
Is your computer network adequate to fit your needs? Are you considering updating any hardware, software, or database modules in the next year?		
Is there anyone in your organization who telecommutes? If so, how is it working out?		
What risks, if any, have you experienced in using your computer system (i.e., viruses, spam, information theft, etc.)?		

PROJECT 18-7: Spreadsheet: Computer Network Communication Costs

This activity is designed to allow you to practice forecasting costs based on percentage of increase over a previous year. After you have completed the following tasks, explain during a class discussion why you think communication costs are such an important expenditure in organizations today and what, if anything, a company can do to contain these costs from escalating so much. Your instructor may ask you to make a formal presentation from your data as a group or individually as well as submit your research for grading.

Complete the following tasks:

1. Retrieve PRJ18-7 from the Data CD; this file contains the worksheet shown below.

2. Use formulas to calculate for each department the new amount of telephone charges based on a forecast that phone costs will increase by 12 percent in the coming year.

3. Create a line graph comparing the actual and projected costs. Use appropriate titles, legends, and grids in your final print.

4. Print the worksheet and the graph in color if you have a color printer.

Department	Actual Jan.-Dec. (Year 1)	Projected Jan.-Dec. (Year 2)
Business Office	$3,692	
Human Resources	$4,000	
President's Office	$1,151	

CHAPTER 19

INTERNET SERVICES AND COMPUTER MANAGEMENT POLICIES

REVIEW ACTIVITY

PROJECT 19-1: Matching Terminology

Directions: In the Answers column, write the letter of the item in Column 1 that is most often associated with each item in Column 2.

Column 1	Column 2	Answers
A. World Wide Web	1. A combination of electronic technology and group processes that supports teams and organizations as they work together and share information over a network.	1. ___
B. Instant messaging		
C. Groupware	2. Symbols used on the Internet to express emotions, a kind of visual shorthand.	2. ___
D. Cookie		
E. E-commerce	3. A small file that a Web server stores on your computer that contains data about you, such as your user name or viewing preferences.	3. ___
F. E-monitoring		
G. Emoticons	4. Verifies that the individual is the person he or she claims to be.	4. ___
H. B2B e-commerce		
I. Intrusion detection software	5. A real-time Internet communications service that notifies a user when one or more people are online and then allows the user to exchange messages with those persons.	5. ___
J. Authentication		
	6. E-commerce that takes place between businesses.	6. ___
	7. Used to identify possible security breaches, such as those committed by hackers.	7. ___
	8. The process of monitoring workers' actions during the workday using a computerized monitoring device or software.	8. ___
	9. A financial business transaction that occurs over an electronic network and includes activities such as shopping, investing, and banking.	9. ___
	10. Consists of a worldwide collection of electronic documents that have built-in links to other related documents.	10. ___

PRACTICAL EXPERIENCE ASSIGNMENTS

PROJECT 19-2: The Environmentalist Is Making Me Crazy!

That's the statement a consultant for International Business Services heard from a client, Mr. Newton, who is operations manager at Ponderosa Paper Co. in Springerville, Arizona. It seems Mr. Newton hired a person who recently became co-chair of the city's Environmental Citizens Task Force. Since becoming co-chair, Mr. Newton says that apparently this "environmentalist" doesn't think the company is doing anything right. The environmentalist has expressed his concerns that: a) the company may be wasting inordinate amounts of paper; b) the computers are not being used efficiently, and c) that the chemicals used in the manufacturing process are being disposed of unlawfully and will eventually adversely affect the environment of Springerville.

Directions: Answer the four questions that follow. You may want to do some additional research about "green computing," which is computer usage that reduces the electricity and environmental waste involved in using a computer. Research two or more large companies in your area and find out how they feel about the above environmental issues. Prepare a paper describing the responses to each question to submit to your instructor. Include the research you have completed in your community and your interpretation of the environmental issues. Be prepared to discuss your findings in class.

1. Identify the real problem in this case.

   _____

   _____

2. What is your solution to the problem you have defined?

   _____

   _____

3. At this point, the environmentalist has only voiced his concern to Mr. Newton. If you were this consultant, would you advise the manager to take these issues to higher management? If so, why?

   _____

   _____

4. In your opinion, what is the responsibility of an organization to address these social issues relative to their computer systems?

   _____

   _____

PROJECT 19-3: *Getting Started and Using Instant Messaging*

This activity is designed to help you install and use Instant Messaging, if you are not already familiar with this communication service. Recall that an instant message (IM) is a real-time Internet communications service that notifies you when one or more people are online and then allows you to exchange messages or files or join in a private chat room with them. Many IM services also can alert you to information such as calendar appointments, stock quotes, weather, or sports scores. Some businesses have found IM preferable to telephone tag for interoffice communications.

Since no uniform standards exist for IM, to ensure successful communications, all individuals on the notification list need to use the same or a compatible instant messenger (i.e., MSN or AOL). If, for example, you are using MSN Messenger, you start like this:

1. *To add friends and family to your contact list:* Simply click Add a Contact to include a friend, relative, or coworker on your list of contacts. Each time you open MSN Messenger, you can see which of your contacts is online and available.

2. *Send an instant message to an online contact.* (A green Messenger icon next to your contact's name in the main MSN Messenger window means he or she is online.)

    • In the main MSN Messenger window, double click an online contact.

    • The Conversation window opens.

    • Type a message in the small box at the bottom of the Conversation window, and then click Send.

Directions: Answer the five questions on the next page, using either your own experience or the experiences your friends have had sending and receiving instant messages. With an awareness of your responses to those questions, write a two-page analysis that describes the effect instant messaging may have on your life and the way business is transacted. Be prepared to discuss your analysis in class as directed by your instructor. You may be asked by your instructor to present a speech in class (using PowerPoint slides or transparencies if available).

1. How often do you IM with friends or persons at work?

    _____

    _____

2. What are the features you like most about IM?

    _____

    _____

    _____

    _____

    _____

3. What are the features about IM that you do not like?

    _____

    _____

    _____

    _____

4. Do you think that a younger person is more apt to communicate using instant messaging than an older person? Justify your answer with facts from your experiences or research.

    _____

    _____

    _____

5. If more people used instant messaging, how would the way we communicate change?

    _____

    _____

    _____

    _____

PROJECT 19-4: *Training Intranet Users in Organizations*

Recall that an intranet essentially is a small version of the Internet that exists within an organization. It has a web server and is accessible via a web browser such as Microsoft Internet Explorer or Netscape Navigator. Users update information on the intranet by creating and posting a web page, using a method similar to that used on the Internet.

Simple intranet applications in organizations include electronic publishing of company materials such as telephone directories, event calendars, procedures manuals, employee benefits information, and job postings.

Directions: Using the form below, interview two companies you are familiar with to learn how they use their intranet capabilities. Evaluate the responses and be prepared to relate your findings in a two-page summary paper to submit and/or to explain during a class discussion as directed by your instructor.

Intranet Question:	Company #1 Name	Company #2 Name
1. Does your organization depend on a company intranet to stay in communication with employees? When and why did you first set up your intranet?		
2. What applications do you make available to employees on your intranet? • telephone directories • event calendars • procedures manuals • employee benefits information • job postings		
3. Are you using the intranet for other groupware applications such as project management, chat rooms, or videoconferencing?		

INTERNET RESEARCH ASSIGNMENT

PROJECT 19-5: E-Commerce Web Sites

This activity is designed to help you analyze and evaluate the effectiveness of electronic commerce web sites from the standpoint of what factors lead to "e-loyalty" or e-commerce customers coming back to do business online with a company.

Complete the following tasks:

1. Retrieve PRJ19-5 from the Data CD; this file contains the table below.

2. Using each of the six factors listed in Column 1, evaluate the effectiveness of the web site according to that factor for three companies of your choice. List the company name at the top of each column. For example, you may want to go to the web sites for Sears, IBM, Dell Computers, Wal-Mart, Amazon.com, L L. Bean, or others of your choice. In the company column, enter your impressions based on each factor represented on the company site.

3. Print a copy of the results. Be prepared to defend your top choice for most "user-friendly web site" in a class discussion led by your instructor. Your instructor may ask that you make a presentation or submit your material for grading.

E-Loyalty Factors	Company #1 Name	Company #2 Name	Company #3 Name
1. Web site appearance			
2. Availability of information			
3. Ease of use or navigation tools			
4. Posted privacy policies			
5. Ease of ordering			
6. Availability of customer service assistance			

HANDS-ON COMPUTER ASSIGNMENTS

PROJECT 19-6: *Word Processing: Groupware and Collaboration*

This activity is designed to review the purpose of groupware and the increased use of collaborative computer activities in organizations today. Recall that groupware is a software application that helps groups of people work together on projects and share information over a network. It enables group members to communicate, manage projects, schedule meetings, and make group decisions. Assume that you are responsible for preparing a flier promoting a training session for employees to learn hands-on how to use groupware features. Your instructor may set a particular size flier for you to design as well as other style features that you should use.

Complete the following tasks:

1. Retrieve PRJ19-6 from the Data CD. This file contains the text that is shown below about the features and functions of many groupware packages. Use this text in your flier:

    - Learn to use:

        - an electronic appointment calendar
        - an address book
        - a notepad
        - a things-to-do list

    - Learn additional ways

        - to stay organized
        - to coordinate appointments and meeting times

2. Design and create your flier using the features on your drawing toolbar. For example, you might want to use some AutoShapes, or textboxes, clip art, pictures, diagrams, WordArt, or other tools that are available on the toolbar. Keep in mind, however, that you want the flier to encourage employees to attend this optional seminar. (Note: Let your imagination go and be creative because there is no right or wrong way to design the flyer.)

PROJECT 19-7: Spreadsheet: Comparison of Market Share

This activity is designed to help you create a simple 3-D pie chart, given the worksheet data. In addition to completing the following tasks, respond during a class discussion, upon the direction of your instructor, regarding the Internet service provider you and your friends use, if you use cable service, or other type of provider. Discuss the reasons you (or someone else) chose the provider you use.

Complete the following tasks:

1. Retrieve PRJ19-7 from the Data CD; this file contains the worksheet shown below.

2. Construct and print a 3-D pie chart. Use appropriate titles, legends, and labels to enhance its appearance and meaning. Show the percentage of each provider next to the appropriate slice on the chart.

3. Print a copy of the pie chart to use during the class discussion and to submit if directed by your instructor for grading.

Market Data As of January — Monterey, California

Provider	Number of Customers
America Online	65,000
MSN	35,000
Earthlink	10,000
CA Access (Local)	9,000
Monterey Cable	42,000

CHAPTER 20

BUSINESS AND COMPUTER INFORMATION SYSTEMS

REVIEW ACTIVITY

PROJECT 20-1: Matching Terminology

Directions: In the Answers column, write the letter of the item in Column 1 that is most often associated with each item in Column 2.

Column 1	Column 2	Answers
A. Data	1. A collection of unprocessed items, which can include text, numbers, images, audio, and video.	1. ___
B. Information Technology Department	2. Resembles a television screen and displays information.	2. ___
C. Information	3. An input device that acts like a miniature photocopy machine that converts an image into a pattern of dots and then transmits the results to a computer.	3. ___
D. Notebook computers	4. Produce paper output in the form of text and graphics.	4. ___
E. Network/server computers	5. An area in the organization that supports and manages an organization's computer-based information system.	5. ___
F. Hardware	6. A device that you can touch on a computer system, such as a monitor, keyboard, or printer.	6. ___
G. Monitor	7. Also known as laptop computers and are small enough to weigh between 4 and 8 pounds.	7. ___
H. Printers	8. Holds data, instructions, and information for future use.	8. ___
I. Storage	9. Data that has been processed and is useful in decision-making.	9. ___
J. Scanner	10. Designed to support a computer network that allows all employees to share files, application software, hardware, and other network resources in an organization.	10. ___

PRACTICAL EXPERIENCE ASSIGNMENTS

PROJECT 20-2: Deciding on a New System Software Package

The offices are buzzing with the possibility that the company is getting a new system software package, the next version similar to Windows® XP. From the employees' standpoint, there is no reason not to upgrade all 50 computers to this new operating system, at a cost of less than $100 per computer. From management's view, however, phasing in this new software is not that easy. Among other things, there's new software to buy (money problem) and retraining (time issues) to be completed.

1. Identify the real problem in this case.

_____

_____

_____

2. What is your solution to the problem you have defined?

_____

_____

_____

3. How does a company decide when to make a change or upgrade its computer system?

_____

_____

_____

4. If the company decided to talk with a consultant, what type of consultant would be best? (Examples: from Microsoft Corp., from the local software store, an outside computer consultant, etc.). Defend your choice.

_____

_____

_____

Directions: Answer the above questions. You may want to interview a few information technology managers to learn how companies in your area decide to upgrade computer systems. What seems to be the norm?

_____

_____

Prepare a paper describing the responses to each question to submit to your instructor. Include the research you have completed in your community. Be prepared to discuss your findings in class.

PROJECT 20-3: Computer Users Committee

This activity is designed to help you determine how computer decisions are made in organizations with computer users committees.

International Business Services has asked you to serve on a newly formed computer users committee consisting of seven individuals. This committee will be composed of workers from each area in the organization. You and other prospective members were told that the purpose of the committee was to discuss issues related to computer and software usage throughout the organization.

At your first meeting, the committee members still didn't have a good idea what to do or where to start in setting up a framework of operations. For the second meeting, you have jotted down three activities/questions that may get the group started. Answer the questions below.

1. Brainstorm what you feel the goals of the committee should be for the first six months.

_____

_____

_____

_____

_____

2. Do you foresee those goals changing after six months? If so, in what ways?

_____

_____

_____

_____

3. What are some advantages to you of being asked to serve on a computer users committee?

_____

_____

Directions: With an awareness of your responses to the previous questions, write a two-page analysis that describes how you think the committee should function. Be prepared to discuss your analysis in class as directed by your instructor. You may be asked by your instructor to present a speech in class (using PowerPoint slides or transparencies if available) describing your leadership style.

PROJECT 20-4: Which Word Processing Software Package is Best?

This activity is designed to help you assess the value of buying one word processing package over another. In any software application (word processing, spreadsheets, databases, etc.), each software package is not exactly the same. Different spreadsheets, for example, may have different methods to enter formulas, use functions, and draw charts.

Word processing software allows users to create a document by entering text or numbers and inserting graphical images, to edit the document by making changes to its existing content, and to format the document by altering its appearance.

Many additional features are included with word processing software. These include: AutoCorrect, AutoFormat, Collaboration, Columns, Grammar Checker, Macros, Mail Merge, Tables, Templates, Thesaurus, Tracking Changes, Voice Recognition, and Web Page Development.

Millions of people use word processing software every day to develop documents such as letters, memos, reports, fax cover sheets, mailing labels, and newsletters. Popular word processing programs include Microsoft® Word, Sun StarOffice® Writer, Corel WordPerfect®, and others.

Directions: Interview two or more persons who use word processing software on a regular basis. Ask each of them the five questions on the next page. With an awareness of the persons' responses to those questions, write a two-page analysis that describes the software packages they preferred and why. Be prepared to discuss your analysis in class as directed by your instructor. You may be asked by your instructor to present a speech in class (using PowerPoint slides or transparencies if available). Use the space below to draft a plan to conduct your interviews. Write the names, addresses, and phone numbers of the two or more persons you plan to interview. Draft a dialogue of how you will ask them to let you interview them for this project.

_____

_____

_____

_____

_____

_____

_____

_____

_____

_____

1. What specific software package do you use? Why?

_____

_____

_____

_____

2. For what purpose is the package used?

_____

_____

_____

_____

3. What do you like about the package?

_____

_____

_____

_____

4. What do you dislike about the package?

_____

_____

_____

_____

5. Would you recommend this software package to other companies to use? Why?

_____

_____

_____

_____

INTERNET RESEARCH ASSIGNMENT

PROJECT 20-5: Notebook Computer Buying Decision

Situation: Use the Internet to research three different computer companies that sell notebook or laptop computers. Assume you are an administrative manager who is looking to find the best deal on a new laptop computer for your company. You have been told to get the most usable features you can for under $1,200. Once you determine which brand best meets the organization's needs, the company intends to buy at least 10 or more of the model you recommend.

Visit Web sites of three computer hardware companies (IBM, Dell, Gateway, Hewlett-Packard, Compaq, or others) and find purchasing information on the features and basic components of notebook/laptop computers.

Directions: Use file PRJ20-5 on your Data CD which contains the table showing the evaluation of basic computer components as shown below. Describe each feature or base component as promoted by the three computer manufacturers. With those ideas in mind, go through a decision-making process of which is the best system to buy.

Describe how you made your decision. Write a summary of the process that you followed. Your instructor may ask you to present your paper along with the information in the table in a class discussion and/or to submit your table and paper for grading.

Base Components	Computer #1 Name	Computer #2 Name	Computer #3 Name
Hard Drive Size?			
Flat Panel Size?			
CD/DVD Bay?			
Pointing Device?			
Operating System Software?			
Application Software?			
Other Storage Devices Included?			
Other Features?			
Total Cost?			

HANDS-ON COMPUTER ASSIGNMENTS

PROJECT 20-6: Word Processing: Evaluation of a Computer Store

This field activity is designed to give you the opportunity to research information for a computer hardware and software purchasing decision and to evaluate a computer store. After you have completed the following tasks, be prepared to discuss which store you would choose to shop for your computer and related software items and why you chose the store you did.

Complete the following tasks:

1. Retrieve PRJ20-6 from the Data CD; this file contains the three questions below. You may choose to use the already-typed questions or to use other questions in your final paper.

2. As a result of visiting a store that sells computer equipment, software, and supplies, key at least two paragraphs responding to the questions. When preparing the copy, use double spacing, and center and boldface the title, "Evaluation of a Computer Store." Your instructor may ask that you present your findings in a PowerPoint® presentation and/or a written paper.

    • What types of computer equipment, software, and supplies are sold?

    _____

    _____

    _____

    • Did a sales representative ask you if you wanted a demonstration on equipment using particular software? Did you have to wait long to get some assistance or to get any questions you had answered?

    _____

    _____

    _____

    • If you had the money and were interested in making a computer-related purchase decision soon, would you buy from this store? Why or why not?

    _____

    _____

    _____

3. Print a copy of your findings in a two-column newspaper format with a line between the two columns. (Hint: Go to the Format menu and select columns.)

PROJECT 20-7: Spreadsheet: Costs of Department Computer Services

This activity is designed to provide practice in allocating costs for computing services supplied to departments by the Information Processing Department in organizations. It's a good idea to have some idea of actual usage in the previous year, so departments can set up their budgets for the new year. In addition to completing the following tasks, explain during a class discussion, upon the direction of your instructor, why you think it would cost more for an information processing operator to prepare a desktop publishing document compared to other types of documents.

Complete the following tasks:

1. Retrieve PRJ20-7 from the Data CD; this file contains the worksheet shown below.

2. Use formulas to calculate the total number of pages processed and the total amount collected for each software used, based on the following scale:

   • Spreadsheet: $4.00 per page

   • Word Processing: $3.00 per page

   • Desktop Publishing: $7.50 per page

3. Bold and italicize the four total lines. Print a copy of the spreadsheet. Be prepared to use your spreadsheet in the class discussion and to submit a copy to the instructor for grading if requested.

Department Name	Software	Pages	Total Cost
Business Office	Spreadsheet	30	
Human Resources	Spreadsheet	12	
President's Office	Spreadsheet	10	
Customer Service	Spreadsheet	21	
Total Cost			
Business Office	Word Processing	10	
Human Resources	Word Processing	92	
President's Office	Word Processing	13	
Customer Service	Word Processing	15	
Total Cost			
Business Office	Desktop Publishing	37	
Human Resources	Desktop Publishing	18	
President's Office	Desktop Publishing	45	
Customer Service	Desktop Publishing	25	
Total Costs			
Grand Total Costs			